AUG   6 2009

D1328595

Divorcing Peacefully:

Why It's Essential and How To Do It

(and How to Co-Parent Successfully After the Divorce)

by

Larry Stone, M.A., MFT

Licensed Marriage and Family Therapist

© *Larry Stone, MFT, 2008*

DIVORCING PEACEFULLY - WHY IT'S ESSENTIAL AND HOW TO DO IT

Copyright 2008 by Larry Stone, M.A., MFT
Licensed Marriage and Family Therapist
Initial publication October, 2008.
Revision 1 published January, 2009

All rights reserved. This book may not be duplicated in any way without the expressed written consent of the publisher, except in the form of brief excerpts or quotations for purposes of review. The information contained may not be duplicated in other books, databases, or any other medium without written consent of the author or publisher. Making copies of this book for any purposes other than your own use is a violation of United States copyright laws.

ISBN 978-0-9820578-1-0
LCCN 2008908359

Published by Bookstone Publishing
P.O. Box 684
Pinole, California
94564
Tel/Fax: 510-964-1200
Publishers website: www.bookstonepublishing.com
Book website: www.divorcingpeacefully.com
Author's main website: www.stonemft.com

Attention: Quantity discounts are available for therapists, attorneys, mediators, family law courts, and organizations dealing with divorce and custody issues.

For more information contact the publisher at the address and phone number above, or email **author@StoneMFT.com.**

About the Author

Larry Stone, M.A., MFT, is a California licensed Marriage and Family Therapist. In addition to individual psychotherapy and couples counseling, he specializes in working with Family Law related counseling issues. He is currently on the approved Evaluator list for Court Ordered Child Custody Evaluations in Contra Costa and Alameda Counties in Northern California, investigates custody for the Family Law Court in high conflict divorces, and writes reports to the Court which include recommendations for custody arrangements. He also meets with couples referred by the Family Law Courts for co-parenting counseling, does private divorce mediation, and serves as a consultant on custody and divorce issues. He is involved with the Collaborative Divorce movement, and strongly believes in the importance of parents working divorce out peaceably, and learning to co-parent together successfully in order to raise emotionally healthy children. He is himself a co-parent, peacefully and effectively sharing custody of his eleven year old daughter.

Acknowledgments:

First and foremost I want to acknowledge the contributions of my clients in helping me to develop an understanding of the dynamics of relationships, divorce, and custody conflicts. Both those who have come to me voluntarily for my assistance, and those who were court ordered into custody evaluation or co-parenting counseling, have each in their own way provided additional understanding of just how relationship conflicts develop, and what happens during the often extreme stress of breakup, divorce proceedings, and custody conflicts. This book could not have been written without them.

I also want to acknowledge Jeffrey Bosshard, friend and attorney, whose gracious assistance in reading and giving feedback on the original manuscript of this book was a significant help in its final development. His philosophy of the need to work together after divorce, and the importance of avoiding saying things during divorce proceedings that would make this more difficult, helped point me in the directions that led to this book's development.

I want to express my appreciation to the staff of the Gottman Institute in Seattle, who were kind enough to read over the paragraphs in which I referred to Dr. Gottman's important work on couples, and give me feedback to insure that his work was accurately portrayed.

I want to thank my friend, Judy Breakstone, for her valuable feedback during the development of my cover design.

Lastly, but definitely not least, I want to acknowledge my own children, who, each in their own individual way, have helped me to better understand the importance of every parent being a present and positive influence in their children's lives, and my youngest child's mother, who, despite our occasional struggles over issues, has learned with me to become an effective and positive co-parent.

I DEDICATE THIS BOOK TO MY DAUGHTER JANELLE, MY YOUNGEST CHILD, WHO HAS SPENT THE LAST ELEVEN YEARS CHALLENGING ME TO BE THE BEST POSSIBLE PARENT I CAN BE, AND INSPIRING ME TO LEARN TO BE AN EFFECTIVE AND COOPERATIVE CO-PARENT FOR HER SAKE.

Contents

Introduction:

As a counselor and psychotherapist, I have worked with many individuals and families contemplating a divorce, going through one, or badly scarred by the one they have recently gone through. After becoming a Court Appointed Child Custody Evaluator, I was able to see a more complete picture of the adversarial divorce process at its very worst, and get a fuller understanding of just how devastating it can be for the entire family. I have also seen that while the divorce might be necessary, the hostility and high conflict often accompanying it never are. Although financial factors (i.e. greed) and personal ideology can be contributing factors to the conflict, the primary reasons for a divorce being high conflict are almost always psychological.

In this book, I will discuss the origins of these conflicts, the often horrendous effects they have on the entire family, and some alternatives that will save everyone involved a great deal of time, money, pain, and stress. Fortunately there are effective alternatives, and they are becoming increasingly more common, but there are still far too many divorces happening at a level of conflict that is both detrimental and unnecessary.

It is my hope that this book will contribute to helping reduce many of these high conflict divorces to manageable proportions, and spare the family members, especially the children, from the negative and painful effects they might otherwise have to live through.

One note here. Throughout this book, I frequently use the term "spouse" or "marital". It is important, though, to recognize that there are many unmarried couples who have a relationship that in all but name may well be substantially the same as a marriage, just without the legal recognition. This would include both male-female couples who, for personal or practical reasons, have chosen to live together substantially as if they were married without making the legal commitment, as well as same sex couples of either gender, many of whom might well have married if the law in their state had allowed them to. Most of what I write here will apply to these couples much the same as to those who are legally married, and they too can make a choice to separate peacefully and resolve their custody and/or property issues together, or fight it out much like married spouses. My use of words implying marriage should not be taken in any way to exclude such couples.

Chapter One: Should Divorce Be A Battlefield?

Why It So Often Is

There are several reasons why divorce often becomes a major battlefield that wounds and traumatizes everyone in the family. One significant factor is the emotional baggage the couple has developed during their marriage. Long before a divorce is contemplated, each spouse has generally collected a substantial number of grievances against the other. There are the times they may have felt neglected, disrespected, treated unfairly or perhaps assaulted. There are all the times they see themselves as having given in to their partner and resented doing so, or felt pushed to the point that they experienced having little or no choice. There are often many instances of behavior they found offensive.

Some of these grievances may be legitimate, but it is my experience that we all see things through our own personal filters that come from our individual life experiences, and all of us have our "buttons" that get pushed. Usually, no one knows better than an angry spouse just which buttons to push and when and how to push them! Even when the grievances are legitimate, they are often mutual, with each party able to extensively enumerate the wrongs the other has committed against them, while being blissfully unaware of their own offenses against the other.

One caveat here. I do not want to ignore the reality that there are some marriages where domestic violence and obsessive control by one spouse leaves the other genuinely helpless and afraid. This is a situation that often does require legal action, including restraining orders and possible involvement by the authorities, and which does not generally lend itself to non-adversarial procedures. It is important to realize, though, that even accusations of domestic violence often come from mutually abusive relationships, where each spouse plays a significant part in the conflicts, and each must be a part of any solution. The vast majority of divorces can be handled in a peaceful and constructive way if both partners truly want that. This is especially important when children are involved. At least one judge has observed that for parents not to have a respectful relationship with each other amounts to child abuse!

By the time divorce is being considered, the sometimes extensive history of each spouse feeling hurt, angry and victimized can result in each feeling intense rage toward the other. Marriages sometimes last far longer than they should, perhaps due to parents staying together "for the sake of the children". By this time, each is likely behaving in ways that act out their anger, whether directly or passively, and by doing so giving their partner more reason for his or her own anger.

Sometimes one of the spouses is unaware there was a problem, and is shocked when the other suddenly asks for a divorce. Although in this situation there may not be the history of angry grievances, at least on the part of the "abandoned" spouse, the feeling of betrayal is often severe, and may well produce an even higher level of conflict. Along with this dynamic is the situation where one of the spouses has gone outside the marriage to be intimate with someone else, one of the most damaging things that can happen in any relationship! I have worked with many couples where both partners actually wanted to try to save the marriage after one had an affair, but the hurt and anger was extremely difficult to overcome, even with genuine motivation. In a divorce, especially if the cheating spouse is leaving their partner for someone else, the feelings of betrayal and the ensuing rage can make any constructive ending to the relationship exceedingly difficult.

Often, whether it comes from a history of built up grievances, the sudden discovery of infidelity or an unexpected desertion, at least one of the spouses feels themselves to be the "victim" and wants retribution. In many high conflict divorces, both spouses feel victimized by the other, and each may want to make the other "pay" for what they see as betrayal of their marital commitments. Even if only one spouse feels like the victim at the time of the breakup, their demands for retribution and retaliation may leave the other with no choice but to fight back to defend themselves.

What I have seen over and over again is that there is seldom a clear cut "victim" in any marital conflict. That is one reason why many states have chosen to have "no fault" divorce laws. Whether I am dealing with a couple trying to salvage and rebuild a marriage or one seeking to end it, the feelings of victimization and the sense of entitlement, rage and desire to retaliate that often go with that, are inevitably destructive and likely to lead to increasingly high conflict and a traumatic divorce scenario. When I am working with such a couple, the most important thing I can do is help them to move out of their sense of victimization and into exploring and understanding the dynamics between them as a couple, including the generally reciprocal nature of relationship conflict. If one or both of the spouses insists on remaining the "victim", then the outlook for any kind of reconciliation or peaceful dissolution is extremely weak, and if either takes the feelings of being the victim into the courtroom, a peaceful and constructive solution becomes unlikely.

There is another factor which is less in the couple's control but which they must still be aware of. When attorneys are hired, they may well buy into their client's perspective, including their feelings of victimization. Even well meaning attorneys can become caught up in their client's hunger to get even. In addition, there are attorneys who will take advantage of the situation, either through ideology or greed, and exacerbate the conflict in unnecessary ways. I will speak in more detail about this issue in the chapter on The Attorney, but let us note here that the attorneys chosen by the spouses can have a considerable influence on the degree of conflict or cooperation in the divorce, and therefore on the amount of pain ultimately experienced by all. For the sake of the entire family, it is essential to be careful in your choice of attorney!

Additional factors which can exacerbate the divorce conflict are the influences of culture and family. If one or both of the spouses come from a background which supports the idea of the victimization of one and blame of the other, then that spouse's personal ideology, as well as their individual support system, may well justify their rage, exacerbate the conflict and encourage retaliatory action. In this scenario, the worst enemy the divorcing couple has can be their well meaning friends and family!

Effects On The Spouses

The high conflict divorce has a negative impact on all concerned. At a time in their lives when the spouses are likely to be in a state of severe stress and depression in the best of circumstances, the addition of high adversarial conflict can exacerbate the hurt and pain, increase the sense of helplessness and depression, and seriously delay the working through and grieving that will let them move on with their lives. This is especially relevant in divorces involving children, where the parents are going to have to work together to co-parent their children, perhaps for many years to come, will have to deal with exchanges when the children will be switching between the parents, may have to coordinate between households with very different rules and values, and will have to somehow find a way to cooperate to make financial and lifestyle decisions that impact their children. These spouses can't walk away from each other after the divorce is final, the way spouses without children can, and the effects of a high conflict adversarial divorce are therefore considerably more severe. It is not incorrect to say that even though spouses can divorce each other, they cannot divorce as co-parents, at least not until their youngest child is at least 18!

Unfortunately, high conflict is much more likely in a divorce with children, where custody and visitation issues are often the source of much of the fighting during the divorce. I will explore this further in the chapter on Custody Conflicts and Custody Evaluations.

The emotional devastation often experienced during and after a divorce, as well as during the preceding period of conflict, is well known as a common, even typical, occurrence. Most people enter into any relationship, but especially marriage, with many hopes and expectations. The failure of the marriage represents a loss not only of the partner and the current living situation, but also of the hopes and dreams the marriage was built on. For many people, it also represents a feeling of personal failure. In addition, it is the beginning of a new stage in life, embarking on some of the most severe changes people go through in their lives, at a time when the individual may have little self confidence, and even less tolerance for any further stress.

This is a time when each spouse needs time to grieve their losses, let themselves heal from the pain, and begin to find ways to move on in their lives. How much more difficult it becomes, then, when this period of great vulnerability is further marked by severe conflict, angry communications and recriminations, and crucial legal battles that each becomes terrified of losing and therefore joins in escalating.

The financial effects can be equally devastating. A single household is already being split into two, with the greater cost associated with that, while the family's income either remains the same, or more likely, is reduced due to time and energy lost through dealing with the divorce. Again, when you add the severe legal battles of an adversarial procedure, this is exacerbated, with more time lost due to Court appearances and other time requirements of the divorce, and less ability to function effectively due to increased stress.

Extended family is also affected by an adversarial procedure. Grandparents and other relatives may find themselves with severely limited access to the children, family members may feel obligated to provide more financial and emotional support than they can comfortably accommodate, and both extended family and friends are often pressured to "take sides", something many may not wish to do.

The greatest detrimental effect of the adversarial divorce, however, is to the children. Except in the most extreme circumstances, children are likely to love both parents, and feel torn apart by not being able to be with both at the same time. The child experiences their world being turned upside down, and generally enters a period of feeling helpless and without any control over their lives. And that is likely to happen even in a peaceful divorce!

Effects On The Children

Imagine how hard it is on the child when his or her parents can't be in the same room without fighting, when exchanges between the parents become times for them to attack each other, when conversations are overheard about Court hearings, restraining orders, supervised visitation, financial struggles, and other matters the child should never be exposed to. It gets even worse when one parent tries to severely limit the child's time with the other parent, often justifying it to the child by the negative things they say about that parent, or complains to the child about how "awful" the other parent is to them. Children are not interested in hearing the negative feelings each parent may have against the other, and should **not** be made a party to the conflict, but all too often that is exactly what happens. The child sees him or her self as part of each parent, and when one parent demeans the other, the children also see it as a negative message about a part of themselves, a painful experience often requiring considerable later psychotherapy to undo.

When a parent feels victimized by his or her former partner, it takes a degree of maturity and awareness of their children's best interest to refrain from expressing those feelings to, or even in earshot of, the children. This is again made worse during a high conflict adversarial procedure, where parents often regress from the combined stressors (parents going through a traumatic divorce are seldom at their best), and may seek to ally with their children against the other parent. The parent is therefore asking their children to take sides, a no win situation for the children.

When both parents push the children to be on their side, and continuously criticize and demean the other parent, the children get the message that in order to please each parent they must hate the other. I am aware of one high conflict case where a young child reported to a court appointed children's attorney that he felt that it was not OK to dream about either parent when in the other parent's house! This is a horrible bind for the child that can be far more traumatic to them than the divorce itself.

Most of the time that a parent tries to alienate their children from the other parent, it simply doesn't work, and if anything alienates the children more from them. The result in these cases is often a child that desperately wants to please both parents, but can't please either without rejecting the other, and so can't win. The child may even learn to appear to be taking sides with the parent they are with, thus creating a "false self" with each parent that makes healthy maturation difficult if not impossible, and telling each parent what they believe that parent wants to hear.

In the worst possible scenario, one parent actually succeeds in alienating the child from the other parent, convincing them to reject the other parent as "bad" and to side with the "victimized" parent. This can result in the child totally rejecting the "bad" parent, even to the extent of refusing contact with them, and therefore being deprived of an important relationship in their lives. The alienating parent may openly support the rejection of the other parent, or may give lip service to the importance of the child seeing the other parent, but then find ways to subtly (or maybe not so subtly) sabotage any connection. This alienation is likely to have a serious and lasting negative impact on the child's emotional growth, and on their ability to form healthy relationships as an adult. It may also result in the child, when they become an adult and realize what was done to them, turning against the alienating parent, possibly permanently. When a parent is found to be blatantly sabotaging their child's relationship with the other parent, they may also have their own custody rights terminated by the court, a risk the alienating parent is likely not aware of. No matter what the outcome, the child always loses!

Studies have been done on the effects of divorce on children, including long term studies following some subjects over a number of years into adulthood. Although every divorce has some negative impact on the children, when the conflict is minimal and both parents arc active in their children's lives, the negative impact is minimized and complete recovery is likely.

When, however, the conflict is high, and parents are unable to communicate or co-parent effectively, the negative outcome for the child is exacerbated, both in severity and in difficulty recovering from the trauma. Acting out behaviors, including those that may result in entanglements with the law, and emotional difficulties, including anxiety and depression, possibly to the point of suicidality, become increasingly likely as the level of conflict escalates. The worst scenario of all is when one parent drops completely out of the child's life. Children seem to instinctively blame themselves for what happens between their parents, and often feel in some way at fault for the divorce. High parental conflict and/or the effective disappearance of one parent, is likely to increase the child's own negative feelings about him or her self, and further lower the child's self esteem, while eliminating one of their main resources for repair. I can't say often enough that no matter what the circumstances leading up to the divorce, the ones who suffer the most from the conflict are the children. The parents may each feel like the "victim", but it is the children who really are!

Chapter Two: Custody Conflicts and Evaluations

Typical Reasons For Custody Conflicts

The most difficult issues to resolve in a divorce, and the ones most likely to result in a high conflict adversarial procedure, often center around the couple's children. After a divorce, parents who were accustomed to seeing their children every day, who, even if they spent the day away at work, knew that the children were there when they got home at night, suddenly face having to share their children with someone who they may feel betrayed and hurt by and furiously angry at, and who they may blame for the entire painful situation in which they now find themselves. The reality is that no matter how big a percentage of custodial time a parent gets, it will be less than what they had before the divorce, and will therefore likely lead to a sense of deprivation. Even a previously absent parent may be jolted by the reality of the divorce, and when suddenly faced with the possibility of losing their children, decide to become significantly more involved. There is simply not enough child to go around when parents suddenly have to share custodial time!

In addition to this sense of deprivation, when there is also a feeling of victimization by the other parent, they may well come to the conclusion that the other parent doesn't "deserve" to have time with "their" children. After all, being asked to share your most precious possession with someone you blame for devastating your life, might certainly seem unfair to most people. These parents don't generally get that the sense of victimization in the marriage is often mutual, and that the problems were more likely about the dysfunctional dynamic that existed in the family than either spouse being a "victim" of the other. More importantly, they often miss the fact that custody and visitation isn't primarily about the parent's right to have time with their children, although that is certainly a real issue, but more importantly about the child's right to have adequate time with each parent!

Another factor that can enter into the conflict is one parent seeing themselves as having been the "primary" parent, with most of the responsibility for taking care of the children, and not wanting that to change. Although more families these days have come to share both income production and child care in the family, there are still many families that, whether by choice or circumstances, are likely to follow the more traditional pattern of one parent (generally the mother) staying home and taking care of the children, with the other parent (generally the father), being the primary wage earner for the family, and doing relatively little direct child care.

When the family breaks up, the caretaking parent may well want to continue what they see as the ongoing arrangement, with them taking care of the children and the other parent paying the bills, but the change in circumstances is likely to result in a change in the other parent also. Faced with the breakup of the family, and the likelihood of seeing their children on only limited occasions and having little influence in their daily lives, the former wage earner may well reorient their priorities in order to make sure they can be actively involved with their children. We seem to have an inborn instinct to fight loss of our children in any way, and that perception of loss is often severe in a parent who, prior to the divorce, spent most of their time as a caretaker. It can, however, be equally severe in a parent who sees themselves as going from being an integral part of their children's family (regardless of the actual time spent with them) to being an occasional visitor with little influence in the children's lives!

Custody Evaluation, The Nightmare Scenario

When a divorcing couple disagrees on custody and visitation arrangements, the Court generally orders them to participate in mediation. The expectation is that, with some help from the mediator, a reasonable agreement can be reached. This happens in the majority of cases. In some jurisdictions, the mediators are "recommending mediators", meaning that if an agreement is not reached the mediator will make a recommendation to the Court. This will normally be, for the most part, implemented by the Court. In other jurisdictions, the mediation is considered confidential, and no recommendation can be made. In these cases, the Court will often keep the current status quo, or some minor variation of it, as a temporary order. In either case, if one or both parents objects to the order that is made, they can dispute the order, in which case the Court, wanting help in determining what is the most appropriate custody solution, is likely to order a full custody evaluation.

A Custody Evaluator, appointed by the Court but paid for by the parents, is ordered to investigate the family and report back to the Court. The evaluation itself is probably like no other experience the family has ever gone through. The evaluator will start by meeting with the parents, either together or individually. He or she will obtain each parent's view of the situation (often getting two stories that disagree on every point), and attempt to develop an understanding of what each parent is asking for and their rational for wanting that. Allegations of one parent against the other are common in an evaluation, as each tries to make their case to the evaluator. These allegations may include neglect, physical or emotional abuse, sexual abuse, substance abuse, or other forms of inappropriate or undesirable behavior.

The allegations are sometimes true, sometimes outright lies, and often based on some element of truth but vastly exaggerated. The parent who feels neglected or abandoned by their ex-spouse will not infrequently project that on the other parent's relationship with their children, and claim the parent is neglectful of the children. This may or may not have any truth to it. I have seen situations where the spouses have absolutely awful relationships with each other and cannot be in the same room without fighting, with each continually giving the other reason to be angry, but where they both have excellent relationships with their children, something each may find extremely hard to believe about the other.

It is the evaluator's job to make sense of these differing stories, competing complaints and allegations, and conflicting demands. In order to write a report to the Court, which normally includes recommendations for the division of custody and visitation, the evaluator must insert him or her self into the family in ways that cannot help but be invasive. Meetings will occur in the evaluator's office with each of the parents, and any potential step-parents that may be involved, both with and without the children, where the person being interviewed will be expected to disclose their complete life histories, or at least any part of that history the evaluator deems relevant. The parents are also being continually evaluated for signs of emotional instability or difficulty in behaving appropriately. When the children are present, the evaluator is carefully watching how the parent relates to them, and how comfortable they are with that parent. These observations will normally count for much more than the (often unreliable) allegations the parents each make about the other.

In addition, the evaluator will likely pay a home visit to each parent, during which he or she will spend at least a couple of hours watching the family in their own environment. Friends and relatives will be contacted and interviewed, as will the children's teachers and day care providers, and any psychotherapists, physicians, hospitals etc. that the family may have had a relationship with. Employers and co-workers may also be contacted. The parents will be expected to sign a release for each of these people to speak with the evaluator, and failure to do so would be considered a lack of cooperation in the evaluation. In other words, the family loses virtually all privacy to the evaluator, and, through the custody report, to the Court. In addition, everything written in the custody report becomes a matter of public record!

The parents generally experience an evaluation as an invasion into their lives, where their privacy is compromised, and they are expected to make themselves available for appointments even when that may mean taking time off work or other inconveniences. Feeling as if they are under a microscope is understandable. In addition to this, the parents are paying the cost of the evaluation, including all meetings and interviews, travel time to home visits, meetings or telephone interviews with various professionals and other contacts, and the many hours necessary to write, edit, and distribute the final report.

When you add the several thousand dollars an evaluation costs to the many thousands likely being paid to two attorneys for consultations, document filing, and court appearances, it is not unusual for the overall cost of a custody evaluation to the family to range from at least $10,000 up to $20,000 and beyond. And that is not including all the other issues the party is likely to take to Court during an adversarial divorce! This is money that could certainly be better spent on making the family's transition to divorce easier, or be put away for the children's future education. An adversarial divorce can result in both spouses starting their new lives in much more difficult financial circumstances than would otherwise have occurred!

It is also important to look at the experience of the children involved. Although what they understand depends to a large extent on their ages, they are certainly aware of being observed by a stranger, both with each of their parents in a strange office, and again with each at home. Older children are generally interviewed, with the level of questioning depending on the age of the children. Although the requests of older children are likely to be given serious consideration, it is common for the children to want to say as little as possible. Children who are old enough to understand what the evaluation is about will know that their parents each consider it important to win, and will often be afraid of doing something that will hurt one parent or the other. Remember, in the vast majority of cases, the children love both parents and DON'T WANT to do anything that will choose one parent over the other, and possibly result on one of the parents they love feeling betrayed by and/or angry at them. For the children, this is a trap, where anything they say could result in unexpected consequences and hurt one of their parents. It is likely to be perceived by the child as a high stakes game with uncertain rules and possibly awful consequences!

How About The Outcome?

Parents often go into an evaluation absolutely convinced they are right, and unwilling to compromise. In these cases, they are sure what the outcome will be. I remember one evaluation where a father, trying to avoid having to go through an evaluation, offered the mother, who was the initial primary parent during the proceedings and had the children with her most of the time, an extremely reasonable balance of custody, one which would have left her as primary parent and given him far less time than he wanted with his children, but which the mother still decided was too much for him to have and therefore rejected.

After observing the quality of the father's relationship with the children (even though he had less parenting experience, the children actually seemed more relaxed with him than with their somewhat overly structured mother), my recommendation, although still leaving the children with their mother more time than with their father, suggested more time for the children to be with him than the mother had turned down before the evaluation! After a lengthy hearing before the judge, during which I was extensively cross examined by the mother's attorney (at the expense of the client), the recommendation was essentially implemented with only very minor changes. A reasonable effort on her part to understand the children's relationship with their dad, and its importance to them, would have spared this family the difficulty and expense of the evaluation, but she appeared too caught up in her own hurt and anger at the father to be able to look at the children's needs objectively.

When the Court is making the decisions regarding the family, the parents have essentially given up control over their own lives. Although the Courts try to find the best possible solution, considering the "best interest of the child" foremost, the decision is still being made by a stranger who, no matter how well motivated, or how well the parents' attorneys present their case, is still deciding with only limited knowledge of the family. Evaluators try very hard to sort through all of the complaints, accusations and demands, and come up with the best possible recommendation to the Court, but they too are human beings who, like everyone else, are not perfect. Likewise the judge, trying his or her best to deal with both the evaluator's report and the arguments made by the competing attorneys, is ultimately creating the court order as a human being with limited access to the realities of the family, and viewed through his or her own experiences and possible unconscious biases.

The family therefore has put its fate in the hands of several strangers, who, no matter how well motivated or how much information they obtain, are still strangers with a limited understanding of the family and all its members.

In any evaluation I do where it seems possible, I will try to get the parents to agree to mediate a solution which they can both accept, and which I can comfortably recommend to the Court. Since this is normally done well into the evaluation, the parents by then have some idea of where it's going, and may well be more flexible than before the evaluation started. I always point out to them that by mediating an agreement, even though they are not getting everything they want, they do have a chance to influence what the final arrangement will be, rather than losing all control. Since the Court will most often implement a stipulated agreement as the order, especially when recommended by the evaluator, the parents doing this usually end up with a far better order for the family than those who fight to the end. They also have a better chance of the order being implemented appropriately by both without the need for further legal action.

This is a considerable improvement over the family fighting to the bitter end, but consider how much time, money and inconvenience was suffered by the family that could have been avoided with good faith compromise and negotiation much earlier in the process!

Chapter Three: The Financial Effects

Attorney's Fees and Court Costs

The cost of litigating a contested divorce can be exceedingly high, often draining the family's assets, possibly causing the sale of the family home, and often leaving the spouses with few assets and sometimes considerable debt to start their new lives apart, instead of having converted those assets into helping each parent get a new start in life and providing for their children's future. A major source of this financial drain is the attorneys' fees. A good attorney (and why would anyone want one that wasn't?) will tend to charge a substantial hourly fee, and will generally bill by the clock for all time spent on the client's behalf, including phone calls, research, time spent on writing and filing forms or in depositions, and of course time spent in court. When the parents are accompanied to court by their attorneys, they are paying for the preparation time for the hearing, time spent getting to and from the courthouse, and time spent waiting for the case to be called (sometimes several hours), in addition to the actual time spent before the judge. Sometimes, due to circumstances, the case could well be postponed to another day, perhaps after everyone has spent several hours waiting to appear. Every minute of this time is being billed for by the attorneys, often at a rate of several hundred dollars an hour. It's not hard to see how this can add up quickly to amounts that go far beyond what the divorcing parties ever expected to have to pay. And, of course, to this must be added the various court fees and other expenses.

Loss of Income

Divorce will often result in a drastic drop in income for the family. This is a result of several factors. Although these factors will exist to some extent in even a negotiated divorce, the high conflict adversarial divorce is likely to seriously exacerbate them.

First of all, let's consider the emotional effects. Since the divorce is a difficult and trying time at best, representing a total disruption of each parent's lifestyle, the end of the dreams and hopes the marriage was based on, and often a sense of failure, it generally becomes a painful and depressing time. There is also the likely need to deal with loneliness, having to find a new place to live (for one spouse for certain, but very possibly for both), and perhaps a drastic change of lifestyle. All of these factors tend to make it difficult to concentrate on work, and make it far more likely that income will be reduced and employment could be in jeopardy. It is hard to function well under this kind of stress at best. Add to the mixture the intense pressure of a high degree of conflict between the spouses, combined with the inevitable anxieties about the possible outcome of an adversarial court case, and it is easy to understand how severe the impact can be on someone's work.

The spouses may find themselves suffering from severe, and possibly debilitating, anxiety and/or depression. This can result in lengthy absences from work, and increase the possibility of loss of employment. There is also the loss of previous support systems. Families may be pressured to side with their blood relative, although it is not unheard of for some families to take the other spouse's side. Friends are torn between the spouses, and often find it impossible to remain friends with both (or may not want to). Couples that the spouses had been friends with as a couple might not be interested in having them come around as a single, which might be seen as a threat to their own marriage. The need to often move to a different location can mean an end to friendly contacts with familiar neighbors, and the need to start making new acquaintances at a time when there are few personal resources for doing so. All in all, the support system is usually greatly diminished. This not only impacts an individual emotionally, but also financially, since there may suddenly be few people in their lives who might watch their children for awhile, possibly no one to turn to for a favor when needed, and the need to pay for services to cover things that might once have been shared between friends.

There is also likely to be an extensive amount of time needed to be taken off work for Court appearances, meetings with attorneys, reading and signing documents, etc. This too can add up and impact the family's financial situation.

As mentioned previously, if the case goes into custody evaluation, there is not only the cost of both the evaluator and many attorney hours related to the evaluation and additional Court appearances, but there are also many hours that need to be taken off work. Courts are in session during the workday, attorneys may only have hours during the parties' normal time to be at work, and the evaluator may need to meet with the family during a weekday, meaning the parent may need to take time off work (and the children may need to miss school). These time requirements also impact the ability of the parents to earn an income.

Forced Sale of Property

A divorce can often result in the family needing to sell the family home and other property. In a peacefully negotiated divorce, it might be possible to work out arrangements that would let one spouse stay in the home and give the other some appropriate compensation, but when the process is highly adversarial, the likelihood of the property having to be sold quickly, even at a loss of potential value, is much greater. Add to this the high costs of an adversarial procedure, and the family's equity in their home may well go to pay the costs of the divorce. At a time when the family is already emotionally devastated, the loss of much of what the family has built financially over the years can add to their insecurity and depression, and make the transition much harder for all.

Strangers Make The Decisions

Each of us, instinctively, wants to have some say in what happens to us, and especially what happens to our children. Much of what the couple may have been arguing about before the divorce is how power and control will be shared in the family. In even the best of divorces, it may be a struggle for each to realize how much less power they suddenly have, and to accept the loss of control in any power sharing arrangement for the future. When the divorce is adversarial, however, the input of each party to the final order is vastly reduced, with a corresponding reduction in influence.

Each will get a chance to tell the Court what they want, but ultimately it is the judge who will decide. In the process of doing this, and trying to find the best solution around the major areas of disagreement, minor issues that may be of importance to one or both parties may well be overlooked, and neither may be happy with the way they are worked out. Although the Court is unlikely to object to changes the parties make themselves by mutual agreement, when they are unable to relate to each other in a productive way, it is very difficult to deal with issues that by themselves might not be highly controversial. In effect, everything becomes an arena to express the conflict and hostility, and neither wants to give in on anything!

The net effect is that the spouses end up with far less control over how things are worked out for the family than they would otherwise have had. An example might be around times of transition for the children to go between the parents, or specifics of sharing holidays. The parents might well be able to come up with a solution that will work better for both than that imposed in the Court order, but if they are unable to negotiate with each other, this will not happen, and they may both be stuck with a schedule that is more difficult for the family than need be.

Chapter Four: The Couple In Conflict

Hurt and Anger

By the time divorce is being considered, the couple has typically descended into frequent (if not constant) arguing, often over small things that once would have been resolved or treated as inconsequential, and each may have become highly skilled at escalating the other. Alternatively, if their style is to withdraw, each has shut the other out to the point where neither feels in any way acknowledged by the other, and both have become bitterly resentful. In some relationships, one partner tends to escalate and the other to withdraw. In these marriages, the escalation of the first partner provokes increased withdrawal by the second, and similarly the withdrawing partner provokes increased escalation with every withdrawal.

Each partner, by this time, is likely to feel extremely hurt by the other, and hurt tends to generate anger. This is especially prevalent with people who do not feel

OK about expressing, or even acknowledging, their hurt, and are therefore likely to move rapidly into rage with little or no awareness of the underlying pain. Many perpetrators of domestic violence follow this pattern, one they may well have learned from their own parents, responding to any hurt or threat with rage as the only way they can permit themselves to express feelings.

With each ensuing battle, the hurt increases, and the angry responses grow in strength, duration, and quickness to appear. Each spouse is more likely to be aware of their own experiences of hurt, abandonment, or attack, and much less likely to empathize with their partner's feelings, which may well be very similar. As the hurt and anger increase, the ability to empathize with or understand the partner diminishes, increasing the perception of being the "victim". (See chapter five below, "Who is the Victim Here".)

Betrayal

People generally marry with considerable hopes and expectations for the future, perhaps naively and unrealistically ignoring the things they should be most aware of about themselves and their partner. The tendency is to not deal with the very things that need to be dealt with, since that would conflict with the idealized "live happily ever after" view of marriage that our culture so fervently supports. When the failure to anticipate and deal maturely with differences in the marriage results in its breakdown, it is not unusual for each partner to feel betrayed by the other.

What has generally been betrayed is actually the idealized and unrealistic view of marriage the partners held, and the naïve expectation they each put on the other to bring them happiness and fulfill their dreams. Nonetheless, the feeling of betrayal is very real, increasing the hurt and anger, and often inciting a desire to "get even". These feelings may be especially virulent in less mature partners, those with a less developed sense of self, who may have invested more of their hopes and dreams in the relationship, and been less able to do the reality testing that would have given them a better perspective on their expectations. People who have sustained severe emotional wounds in childhood may be particularly vulnerable to this, tending to judge their experiences through the filters of their childhood pain, and often projecting once familiar expectations on their current partner.

This "natural" sense of betrayal, likely common to most marital breakups, is severely exacerbated by either of two highly destructive circumstances. One is where one partner had no idea the other was unhappy in the marriage, and experiences a feeling of being completely blindsided by that partner leaving or requesting a divorce. For this to happen usually requires participation by both partners, one of whom withholds and withdraws, not talking about his or her unhappiness when it might still be possible to deal with it constructively, while the other chooses not to see what they don't want to see, cooperating in the avoidance. The marriage thus develops its own "don't ask, don't tell" policy, much to its detriment.

The second situation is where one partner has "gone outside the marriage", having a relationship with another. Generally it is a sexual relationship that brings on the betrayed feelings, although I have seen couples struggling with "emotional infidelity" with the same intensity as if it had been physical.

Whatever the reasons for the feelings of betrayal, and regardless to what extent those feelings may or may not be justified by reality, the "betrayed" spouse is often consumed with feelings of vengeance, wanting to somehow "get even" for what has "been done" to them. Many a family law attorney has profited handsomely from representing a "betrayed" spouse, or their partner who may be fighting desperately to avoid losing their children or being financially destroyed by the divorce.

Judgment, Criticism and Blame

In the diversity of modern society, where it is the exception rather than the rule to find partners who have grown up in identical environments, perhaps knowing each other and each other's families since childhood the way one might expect in an agrarian society, virtually every marriage is a cross cultural one. This may be obvious when there are clear ethnic or racial differences, but even when the couple, to all outward appearances, seems to be from the same culture, they are likely to have grown up differently, often in families with vastly different values and expectations, and may have received very different messages from friends and peers as to what marriage "should" be.

When a couple approaches marriage with maturity and an openness to learning about, understanding and validating their partner, and when they can accept and honor their differences and negotiate compromises when necessary, the marriage is likely to work well. All too often, however, there is a tendency for each to see their way of doing things as the "right" way, and to be critical of the other for being "wrong".

This kind of critical attitude, if not promptly dealt with, can wear away at a relationship until there is little left. In any relationship, there are times each person might feel critical of the other, but what is important is how it is handled. If the criticism is presented respectfully, the one feeling critical owns their feelings as being their view of the world rather than an absolute truth, and the one receiving the criticism is not hypersensitive to it, then the substance can be discussed and negotiated. Two people in a relationship certainly don't have to like, or even approve of, everything the other does. If, however, each treats the other with contempt and disdain, acting as if there is something "wrong" with the other, or neither is able to accept responsibility for their own actions and how they affect others, then the relationship is likely doomed.

John Gottman and The "Four Horsemen"

Dr. John Gottman is a well known psychologist who has done considerable research into couples in conflict. Along with his wife, Julie Gottman, he has observed and filmed many couples, has studied their interactions, and has become able to predict with a high degree of accuracy whether or not their conflicts are likely to lead to a breakup of the marriage. He states that couples that stay together may well argue as much as those that break up, but it is *how* they argue that makes the difference!

The couples that get through their fighting and make their relationships work tend to fight about issues, not about each other. Gottman has defined what he calls the "Four Horsemen of the Apocalypse" of couple relationships. They are *criticism, defensiveness, stonewalling,* and *contempt.* When he observes couples using these in their arguments, he is able to predict with considerable accuracy that they will eventually break up. Those who argue about issues, but without any evidence of the "Four Horsemen" are likely to get past their conflicts and stay together. In addition, he has stated that in healthy, long lasting relationships there are far more positive and supportive interactions than negative ones, with a minimum of a 5 to 1 ratio (positive to negative comments) during conflict discussions and at least 20 to 1 outside of conflict discussions. In couples who are not happy, the ratio is far lower, both during and outside of conflict discussions. The lower the ratio, the more likely that the relationship is in trouble and there will be an eventual breakup. I will address each of the "Four Horsemen" below.

1. Criticism:

When we criticize our partners, rather than just disagreeing with them, we are making the argument personal. There is a tremendous difference between disagreeing with someone with respect, letting them know that our needs, preferences or values are different than theirs and we would like a different solution to whatever problem exists, or criticizing them, telling them how "wrong" they are. Criticism comes from a "one-up" position, and partners who are critical often act like an angry parent, treating their partner as if he or she were a disobedient child that needs to be corrected. When criticism is seen in this perspective, it becomes obvious why it often leads to escalated conflict. Criticism might well provoke responses such as defensiveness or passive-aggressive behavior, and in some relationships a dynamic develops of parent-like criticism on the part of one partner, and childlike defiance on the part of the other, each part of this dynamic escalating the other in a "chicken and egg" pattern. In other relationships the criticism is mutual, each partner acting like the "critical parent" toward the other, and each escalating their criticalness in response to the other's criticism.

2. Defensiveness:

We might all sometimes feel defensive if we believe we are being falsely accused or unfairly criticized. When, however, any statement by one person that they disagree with something another has done, said or wants results in a defensive response, and an individual is unable to take any responsibility for the part they might be playing in a conflict, then the degree of defensiveness becomes a serious problem. Difficulties in a relationship are worked through by honest communication, and that requires each partner to make an effort to hear, understand and relate to the other's perspective, as well as to own the part they might be playing in the conflict.

When someone responds to any such communications with rationalization, blaming, or counter-criticism, it short circuits the communication process necessary to negotiate and resolve the issue and move past it to reconnection and genuine intimacy. A typical defensive response might be, when one partner brings up something that bothers them, the defensive partner immediately responds by telling the first partner what _they_ did wrong, somehow justifying their own behavior and invalidating their partner's concerns. Defensiveness may well result in the other partner either trying harder and harder to get through, until a loud argument results, or withdrawing and effectively giving up on any communication.

3. Stonewalling:

If one partner refuses to talk about an issue, avoids any attempts to discuss it, or quickly changes the topic to something more comfortable, the issue never gets resolved. Unresolved issues tend to linger and build up. If one partner is trying to resolve the issue, whether through healthy communication or otherwise, the experience of being "stonewalled", is likely to leave them feeling shut out and ignored, and provoke increasing resentment. This often results in progressive escalation, where the stonewalled partner tries ever harder to get heard, increasing their attempts to communicate, perhaps getting pushier, louder or more critical, and the stonewalling partner responds to this by increasing their withdrawal and avoidance. If, on the other hand, both partners tend to stonewall, issues never get brought up, and the relationship is likely to die a quiet death of bitter resentment by both. What is truly unfortunate here is that the issues themselves might well have been easily resolved if they had only been discussed!

4. Contempt:

This is perhaps the worst form of interaction in a relationship, and is an almost certain harbinger of eventual disaster. When one or both of the partners treats the other with contempt, uses name calling and "put downs", responds disdainfully to whatever the other says or does, and generally tries to diminish the other rather than simply disagree and negotiate with them, then the relationship is on a steep slide to an acrimonious ending. No one likes to be treated contemptuously, and those who are treated so are likely to develop rage and even hatred toward their partner. In some highly dysfunctional relationships, both partners treat each other with contempt, rapidly escalating the imminent destruction of the relationship.

Desperation and Despair

The degree of conflict generated by the time divorce or separation is discussed, and the hurt, feelings of betrayal and sense of failure that often accompany a breakup, may well leave one or both of the parties feeling desperate. They are likely to be facing severely diminished financial circumstances, loss of time with their children, being cut off from much of their former support group, and feelings of rejection and isolation. This is not uncommon in a marital split, and may well lead one or both of the parties to a state of despair.

People feeling desperation and despair are seldom able to act rationally. They may resort to self destructive behaviors (drugs, alcohol, poorly chosen relationships, compulsive behaviors, domestic violence) and make choices they would not have made in a more rational state. These choices might well exacerbate the conflict between the partners, and/or create additional stress on the children. It is often at a time like this that one or both of the parties is likely to seek out a "barracuda" type of attorney, or be vulnerable to one who pushes them to "get" the other party. I will address the issue of attorneys in Chapter Six.

Chapter Five: Who Is Really The Victim?

Inevitable Feelings of Victimization

In thinking about the dynamic that may have developed between the couple, it is not hard to imagine each one seeing themselves as the "victim" in the divorce. Each is best able to see what their partner has "done" to them (or ways in which they have been neglected), and finds it much more difficult to see the role they themselves have played, the hurts, betrayals and neglects they have perpetrated on their partners.

With relatively mature individuals, the sense of betrayal may initially be there, but they will likely be able to get past it to a point of recognizing at least some of the mutuality, essential for constructive dialogue. When the partners are less mature, and perhaps have themselves come from highly dysfunctional families, they may well get stuck in their sense of victimization. In virtually every couple in conflict I have worked with, whether they have come to me for counseling to repair their relationship, divorce mediation, co-parenting counseling, or, in the worst case scenario, custody evaluation, each has played a part in the conflict, and each must play a part if there is to be any healing. In my experience, the relationship where there is one "innocent victim" and one "evil perpetrator" is rare.

The reality is that no matter how much one or both partners see themselves as the victim, they most likely have each played a part in creating the problem. The only "victim" in a typical divorce is the children, who are never to blame for their parents actions (although they may often blame themselves), and who suffer the most by the breakup.

Retaliation and Retribution

One common occurrence when there is a feeling of being victimized is a desire to retaliate and "get even". When we feel hurt and betrayed by someone, it is only human to want to strike back, perhaps to "make him or her feel the way I feel". Unfortunately, in a relationship breakup, this feeling will only tend to exacerbate the conflict. When you have two partners who each feel betrayed and victimized, and who each want to get even with their former partner, then the stage is set for continually escalating conflict. Each retaliatory act by one partner increases the feeling of victimization by the other, giving them in turn more to retaliate for. Even if only one of the partners is in a retaliatory mode, their actions will tend to be counterproductive, and the other partner, in self defense, is likely to fight back.

Negative Expectations and Reciprocating Cycles

With a partner who is being retaliatory, we will learn to expect a negative, counterproductive, and often painful response to whatever we do, even when we might be trying our best to be appropriate and avoid conflict. Inevitably, we will begin to change our actions in anticipation of being attacked. In this situation we get little or no payoff for responding positively, and therefore might well find it hard to be motivated to continue to do so. When each partner is retaliating, then the negative expectations on both sides will have a basis in reality, providing a feedback loop that will tend to encourage increased hurt, anger and conflict.

This creates a reciprocating cycle. Each action by either partner results in the other feeling attacked, and produces an escalated response. After a certain point it becomes impossible for the two to be in the same room for even a short time without fighting, or even to be on the phone together peaceably. Courts will sometimes order the parties in an adversarial procedure to communicate only by email, but even this can become an arena to further the conflict. When the situation reaches this point, it is difficult for the couple to work out any reasonable accommodations, often resulting in a brutal, painful and expensive divorce.

Children, The Real Victims

The only real "victims" in this situation are the children. Although meeting a child's needs can be stressful and add to the difficulties the couple is experiencing, the child is simply behaving like a child. It is the parents' job to find how to meet the child's needs in order to fulfill their role as parent, as well as to find the support they need to help their own functioning. The stress that parenting can add to a relationship should never be blamed on the child!

In all but the most severely abusive or neglectful situations, children inevitably love both their parents, and feel hurt and angry when the parents separate.

Although older children might be better able to logically understand the need for the divorce, that doesn't mean they can ever be complacent about it. Their world revolves around both their parents, and it inevitably is being sundered by the break in their parents' relationship.

In even the best of circumstances, children will be painfully impacted by a divorce. If, however, the divorce is handled peacefully, both parents stay highly active in the children's lives, and the children experience them as being able to co-parent cooperatively for the children's best interest, then the damage is minimized, and the children will most likely work through their loss and be able to develop with relative normalcy. When the conflict is high, however, the actions the parents are likely to take will impact their children in negative and painful ways.

Experiencing that the two people they love and need the most can't get along with each other is confusing and painful. If the parents are highly critical of each other, to or in front of the child, this increases the damage to the child. Sometimes parents will refrain from actively talking to the child about the other parent, but will talk freely in earshot of the child, without any thought of the effects on the child of what is being overheard. Even worse is when the parent actively tells the child how "awful" the other parent is. A parent who feels abandoned by their partner might tell the child that the partner is abandoning the child also, although this might not be in any way true. In the worst possible scenario, one parent tries to actively alienate the child from the other parent, trying either openly or surreptitiously to get the child to take their side and treat the other parent as their "enemy" also.

Parental Alienation

Attempts to alienate children from their other parent are not only unfair to that parent, regardless of the relationship between the adults, and not only likely to lead to vicious and expensive court battles, but are also extremely destructive to the children, likely causing serious and possibly permanent psychological and developmental damage. Most of the time, the efforts to alienate children do not succeed, but result in the child feeling alone and unsupported, and possibly more distant from the alienating parent.

This can produce a depressed and anxious child, very possibly one who acts out destructively.

In the instances where the alienation succeeds, the results are even worse. If the child buys into either parent's story of victimization and chooses to shut out the other parent, possibly even refusing to have contact with them despite any court orders to the contrary, the child loses one of the most important relationships in their life, and carries with them the burden of their choice, possibly for the rest of their lives. When children are alienated from a parent who wants to be active in their lives, this is in itself a form of child abuse!

Sometimes, parents will have the illusion that a step-parent will substitute for the alienated parent. This is simply not true. Although a step-parent who is loving, caring and supportive to the child and can serve as a good role model is helpful, no matter how good the step-parent is, he or she will never substitute to the child for their own missing parent. If a parent has chosen to drop out of their child's life, or a child has been alienated from that parent, then having a loving step-parent or other supportive figures of the missing parent's gender in the child's life will help, but it will never fully make up for the missing parent. In fact, it is essential to not introduce a new "substitute parent" into the family too soon, ***or too often***!

Chapter Six: The Attorney

"Zealous Advocacy" - Surviving Your Attorney!

The guidelines for attorneys instruct them to represent their clients with "zealous advocacy", in other words to work to get the best possible solution for their client. This is true not only in family law, but in any form of legal representation, whether civil or criminal. Like anything else, however, how this is interpreted in practice can vary widely.

I can remember an attorney I know, a friend for many years, once telling me that in family law, he would never say or do anything in court that would make it more difficult for the couple to co-parent together in the future. Although representing his clients and working to make sure their interests are fairly put forth, he also expects his clients to accept a reasonable solution, one which protects their interests but is fair and appropriate, rather than going for all he or she can get. This is a wise attitude, and one which, in the ideal world, all family law attorneys should have. This interpretation of "zealous advocacy" involves looking at the long term best interest of both the client and their children!

The "Barracuda"

Unfortunately, not every attorney sees this the same way. There are attorneys who believe that the ethical way to represent their client is to go for everything they can get. If their client is the custodial parent, they might try to severely limit the children's access to the other parent, often looking for any excuse to discredit the other parent and prove him or her unworthy of being with the children. If their client is not the primary custodial parent, they might fight to take over custody of the children, whether or not that is actually in the children's interest, similarly looking for any way to discredit the custodial parent. It is not unheard of to find false allegations of molest, substance abuse, violence, neglect etc., perhaps coming out of the fantasies of the "betrayed" parent, but encouraged and exaggerated by their attorney.

Likewise in the financial arena, the attorney representing the parent likely to get support might try to milk the supporting parent for all they can, perhaps to the extent of leaving them without enough funds to survive themselves, while the attorney representing the client who might have to pay support may try to drastically minimize the support to be paid, even if it leaves the other parent destitute.

This attitude may be the product of ideology on the part of the attorney. A radical feminist, seeing women as victims and men as invariably to blame, might well fight to get everything for their female clients without any regard for the long term harm to the family. Likewise, the male equivalent, who is angry at the way the family law system has at times favored women, might well be dedicated to "reversing" this and turning the tables, again without any regard for the harm it might bring to a particular family.

The Profit Motive

In discussing the "barracuda" attorney, we unfortunately can't ignore the profit motive. Although the practice of law, despite the often humorous stereotypes, is filled with many ethical and reasonable attorneys, who put fairness and the long term interest of their clients and the clients' children first, there are some who fight with overly much zeal for their clients out of recognition that it is in their (the attorney's) best interest to do so. When one attorney tries to "go for the jugular" in a family law case, rather than for a fair and reasonable solution, then the other party has little choice but to hire someone who can fight back with equal vigor, even if that might not be their preferred style. As might be expected, the net result of this is increased conflict, and many hours spent in court, fighting over one thing after another. An attorney like this will line their own pockets, but might well leave both parties to the divorce with little money left to reestablish their lives or provide for their children's future, and with intense anger at each other that may interfere with healthy co-parenting for years to come.

Importance of The Attorney's Philosophy

As you probably realize by this time, if a divorcing couple is choosing to hire attorneys, the philosophy of the attorney can make a significant difference in their lives. Even most ethical attorneys will refer to those who are overzealous in what they demand and/or their attacks on the other party as "barracudas". It is a term I have heard ethical attorneys use with disdain and marked disapproval when referring to some of their less ethical colleagues.

When someone seeking a family law attorney is feeling desperation and despair (see Chapter Four), they may be highly vulnerable to the influence of a greedy or ideologically fanatical attorney. Here is where it becomes extremely important to keep one's ultimate goals in mind. A fair settlement which lays the groundwork for a healthy co-parenting relationship, will always serve the family, and especially the children, better than an expensive and brutal high conflict adversarial divorce! An attorney who will help protect their client against an unfair judgment, but will refuse to participate in a winner take all strategy and instead provide their client with appropriate reality testing, is **always** a far better choice than one who is willing to fight for unreasonable demands and exacerbate the conflict unnecessarily!

Chapter Seven: So What Are The Options?

The Four Styles of Handling A Divorce

There are several options for divorcing, essentially divided into four categories, of which the adversarial divorce is one. As you probably gather by now, that is almost always the worst possible option, and one to be seriously avoided if at all possible. So what are the others? They fall primarily into three categories, the do-it-yourself approach, sometimes known as the "kitchen table" divorce, mediated divorce, and collaborative divorce. I will discuss all of these options below.

The "Kitchen Table" Divorce.

The least expensive form of divorce is one in which the parties negotiate all issues themselves, draw up an agreement, and file it "Pro Per" (without an attorney). This can work well if there is very little to argue about, in other words there is little or no estate to be divided, no alimony to be paid, and there are no children in the picture. However, as soon as one of these factors or any similar issue with potential contentiousness enters into the picture, the situation changes drastically.

There is a famous saying that "A verbal contract isn't worth the paper it's written on". This is very true for any issue that could potentially be decided in a court of law. Although a do-it-yourself divorce is clearly negotiated with the idea of avoiding that, issues can come up later in ways that were not anticipated. Only by having a clear and fully defined agreement can this be avoided, one that leaves little room for disagreement no matter what comes up. If, for instance, a couple is working out a custody agreement on their own, it might work well until one parent wants to move, or gets involved with a new partner, or some unexpected issue comes up where the two parents disagree strongly about how to raise their child. Then, unless their agreement has anticipated and allowed for future disagreement, the previously peaceful divorce may turn into a high conflict post-divorce battle as their differences "hit the fan".

Need For A "Fallback Position"

It is not unheard of that one parent, at some time in the future, has either a religious or ideological conversion, gets involved with a new partner with different values, has a change of circumstances in their life, or for some unknown reason suddenly wants to change not only their own lifestyle, but how their children are raised. One parent might make some significant lifestyle changes that the other strongly disapproves of, or get involved with a partner the other thinks is inappropriate. A parent who thought that he or she was OK with the agreed on arrangements may suddenly develop "buyer's remorse". Financial situations may change, resulting in one parent wanting to change a financial settlement that previously had seemed OK, and the other disagreeing. Whatever the specifics, suddenly one parent decides that the informal agreement that was in place is no longer suitable, and wants to make changes that the other won't agree to.

This doesn't mean that the parents have to rigidly adopt the terms of any agreement. When I work with a couple developing a co-parenting perspective, I will encourage them to be as flexible as possible, for each to offer to cover time for the other when needed (but not to take advantage of each other), to allow each other extended vacation times with the children when requested, to offer or request reasonable tradeoffs in time or responsibility when appropriate, etc. What a clear and specific agreement does is create a **fallback** position that takes over when the parents can't agree, and essentially provides boundaries for their relationship. This actually makes negotiation and cooperation easier and more likely, since each parent knows that if they don't respond positively to requests by the other parent, they cannot expect their own requests to be honored, and each understands the limits of their own power. Over a period of time, with each parent responding this way even if only out of self interest, working together becomes a habit, with positive consequences for the entire family. The combination of a very specific fallback position spelled out in the agreement, and a willingness to be flexible with each other in reality, is the best way to ensure peaceful co-parenting throughout the children's developmental years. This is why even parents who can negotiate an agreement on their own would still be best off getting help from a qualified professional!

It is doubtful that the "kitchen table" divorce will lay a groundwork that can be applied to future contentious issues that might not have been foreseen at the time it was drawn up. The couple has generally worked hard to avoid conflict, and neither partner is likely to bring up potential areas of disagreement that are not actually happening at the time. A professionally developed agreement, although it might not anticipate some of the things that can happen, will be clear and explicit about what the rights and responsibilities of each parent are, who gets to decide what, how much time the children are with each parent, etc. Although nothing can stop a litigious ex-partner from suddenly deciding to bring legal action, having a clearcut and decisive written agreement, one which provides a clearly set bottom line fallback position, will make that action much less likely, and would make the status quo of the agreement significantly more likely to be adhered to by the court if it should be contested.

Mediation

Mediation is the least expensive and least contentious approach to having a divorce agreement arrived at professionally. A trained mediator may be either an attorney or a licensed psychotherapist, but in addition to the standard trainings in their field, they have undergone considerable training in the art of professional mediation. Unlike couples counseling, in which a primary emphasis might be on improving communication and healing the relationship, the mediation is primarily focused on working out the specifics of an agreement that both parties can accept. The mediator will give each party a chance to state what they would like in an agreement, will help them explore areas where they disagree, and guide them in coming up with negotiated compromises.

This does not mean that work can't be done in a mediation process to help smooth out communications between the parents. It is often helpful, and sometimes essential, to work with the parents' styles of communication and negotiation to facilitate the mediation. What it does mean is that the emphasis is in a different place, more on reaching specific agreements, and less on the dynamics of the parents' interactions.

For some couples, the process of negotiation is comfortable, and they recognize the need to compromise. For others, it is more difficult, and compromise comes harder. Sometimes each feels justified in demanding their position; then it is up to the mediator to help them get past the place of being stuck and become able to explore other options. I will discuss ways in which the mediator can do this below, when I talk about the different types of mediators and approaches to mediation.

As the mediation progresses, the mediator will write down the issues, list the solutions agreed to, and keep track of issues still to be resolved. When an agreement is reached, the mediator will likely draw it up formally, ready to be signed by the parties. If the mediator is an attorney, he or she might file the agreement on behalf of one of the parties. When the mediator is a therapist, the parties will need to either file it themselves (Pro Per), or take it to an attorney to be attached to a formal filing. As a therapist-mediator, I always inform my clients that they have the option of having an attorney look over the final agreement before signing, even if they intend to file Pro Per. This can help them feel more confident that their rights are being protected. I will address below the advantages and disadvantages of using either an attorney-mediator or a therapist-mediator.

There are some conditions necessary for mediation to be an option for handling a divorce. First of all, even if the parties are still angry at each other, they have to be able to sit calmly in the same room without descending into explosive conflict. While a mediator can do a great deal to help calm their clients and encourage the mediation process, we are still limited by what we have to work with. If one or both clients are unable to get past their anger enough to discuss and negotiate issues, mediation simply cannot be made to work.

No matter how much one or both clients may feel themselves to be the "victim", a mediation cannot be used as a venue for revenge. It is the rare client indeed who would allow themselves to be talked into a lopsided agreement that serves the interests of vengeance more than that of fairness, and an incompetent mediator who would assist in promoting such an outcome. For mediation to be successful, both parties must understand that compromise is necessary, sometimes compromise which seems painful. They must be willing to accept less than what they ideally want, and possibly less than they believe they should have. If they are able to understand that the other party is having to do the same, this can make it easier to arrive at a difficult compromise.

Attorney or Therapist?

The first decision to make in choosing a mediator is whether to use an attorney or a therapist. Keep in mind that either one will have been trained in mediation, but they bring different strengths to the table.

The attorney-mediator should be well versed in the legal traditions of the jurisdiction, what the courts expect, what judges would consider acceptable, and what may be the likely outcome of an adversarial procedure. This knowledge can be helpful in arriving at an agreement, especially with parties who put a great deal of emphasis on the legal technicalities. Additionally, an attorney who is experienced in estate law might also be helpful in working through the division of a large and complicated estate with considerable assets.

The therapist-mediator is likely to be an expert on communications, and may well be able to do more than the attorney to lessen the level of conflict, facilitate productive communication, and help the parties to understand each other's needs and arrive at a compromise that genuinely feels acceptable to each. The therapist is also more likely to have knowledge of child development, and the needs of the children in determining a custody arrangement. When I am contacted about a divorce mediation, I inform the prospective clients that as a therapist and custody evaluator, I am able to provide extensive assistance to them in mediating the custody aspect of the dispute, and can help them work out compromises on simple financial issues, but make it clear that if there is a large or complex estate which they disagree about they may also need to involve an attorney or other financial expert to assist with the estate. Although this will result in an additional expense, the hourly cost of a therapist-mediator is generally significantly less than that of an attorney-mediator, normally resulting in lower cost even when there is a need to involve another professional for part of the process.

There are also different approaches to mediation, ranging from passive to very active, and it is important to find an approach that matches your own personality. In the passive approach, the mediator's role is primarily to facilitate communication between the parties, and he or she does not provide any input about a possible solution, make any suggestions or recommendations, or support any position or suggestion by one of the parties. One example of this approach is mediation by someone trained by the Center for Non-Violent Communication. In this approach, the mediator helps each party to get in touch with and express the genuine needs underlying their positions, and to explore letting go of those positions and looking at options that meet each one's needs.

The positive side of this approach is that it can often improve the ongoing relationship and communication between the parties, which is especially important when there are children involved and the parents will need to co-parent cooperatively with each other, sometimes for many years. The problem with it, however, is it is likely to work best with parties who are realistic and do not tend to be rigid about their positions. Unfortunately, in the typical divorce situation, where the parties are likely going through considerable emotional turmoil and stress, this is often not the case. When one or both of the parties resists letting go, this is an approach which can flounder, can drag on for a long time with little progress, and may be unlikely to help them arrive at an agreement.

I personally prefer a more active approach, where the mediator is also an expert in the field, and willing to function in the role of consultant as well as mediator. I will make it clear to my clients that as a therapist who has worked with the Courts and can bring to the table a knowledge of both children's developmental needs and the kinds of agreements the Court is likely to support, that if I believe one party is being unreasonable or unrealistic, I will tell them so. I will also participate actively by suggesting (and supporting) possible solutions that I believe will best meet both the parents' needs and the children's. Although a goal of mediation should be to help the parties arrive at compromises they can both be comfortable with, not every compromise has to be exactly in the middle between what each is asking for, especially if one of the parties may be being more realistic than the other in what they ask. Helping parties that seem stuck to create a realistic and workable agreement, even if it is not what either had originally envisioned, is a positive outcome, and, in my opinion, far better than just creating good communication that lets them continue to struggle with irresolvable positions. It is also important to remember that few children keep track of the details of their parents' time sharing as long as they get to have significant time and a good relationship with each!

"Buying In"

When a mediation is successful, the final outcome is normally far better than a solution ordered by the Court. This is true even if the order is essentially the same as the mediated result! With a Court ordered solution, at least one of the parties is likely to feel unfairly treated and be left with considerable resentment. Ironically, it's not unusual for *both* of the parties to feel this way. The result of this is often minimal compliance, given reluctantly and with considerable resentment. Depending on the level of functioning of the parties, it may also result in increased arguing, passive aggressive actions designed to sabotage or get even, and ongoing conflict. It is well known that the time immediately after the decree is issued is often the most difficult for the divorcing parties, and it is not unusual for a high conflict adversarial divorce to have legal battles that go on year after year, *or at least until the money runs out*.

When the agreement is mediated, both parties have some investment in the solution, and make a commitment to follow its provisions. Although each may feel some unhappiness over what they did not get, each has also had some say in crafting the agreement, and has gotten at least some of what they wanted. In addition, a well written mediation agreement will look at foreseeable future changes, have some provision for when and how they might be handled, and create an effective "fallback position" that holds until the parents can reach agreement on those issues. This provides significant help in reducing the likelihood of future Court battles.

This kind of arrangement is not only helpful to the parents themselves, but is especially important for the children involved, who are depending on their parents to continue parenting them, are likely dealing with abandonment and rejection issues in the best of circumstances, and are typically highly sensitive to how their parents are cooperating and communicating after the divorce.

Collaborative Divorce

There are many couples who may not have the trust or willingness to cooperate with each other necessary for mediation to succeed, but still want to avoid the expense and high conflict of an adversarial divorce. There is a relatively new alternative for these couples called Collaborative Divorce. Although more complicated and expensive than a simple mediation, it is usually far less so than an adversarial procedure, and results in the same positive results as mediation: lessened conflict, a sense of having been at least part of the solution and gotten at least part of what they want, and an improved ability to co-parent cooperatively. This approach is becoming increasingly recognized by various legal jurisdictions, which until now have been designed primarily around the adversarial concept, which many attorneys and judges feel extremely frustrated with when applied to family law. It is my belief that collaborative divorce will become more and more popular over the next couple of decades, possibly to the extent that it may well become the expected method of resolution in many jurisdictions.

The collaborative process involves a team approach. Each party has an attorney, but one who has received collaborative team training and who is committed to finding a cooperative rather than adversarial solution. Each party also has a divorce coach, who is a qualified, licensed therapist who can help provide support through this difficult time, as well as reality testing when their client is being unreasonable or vengeful, or begins getting stuck in their positions. In addition, if there are children involved, a child specialist is brought in to be the voice of the children. This is a therapist familiar with children's development and needs, and able to talk to the children and present their needs and preferences to the parents and the collaborative team. A financial specialist is also generally brought in, especially if there is any considerable value to the estate to be divided. Each of these professionals has undergone the full collaborative team training, and is prepared to work together with the rest of the team to help create a solution for the family.

One of the elements that makes Collaborative Divorce different than an adversarial one is the contract the parties and team members sign. In addition to permitting the members of the collaborative team to communicate freely with each other regarding the case, meaning there will be no confidentiality for the parties between members of the team, (normal rules on confidentiality would, of course, apply to any communications from a team member to anyone *outside* the team), they also agree that if the collaboration does not succeed and one of the parties decides to go to Court, the entire team will resign, and the attorneys that have been part of the collaborative process will not be able to represent them in Court in any future adversarial procedure. This means that the parties would have to restart with new legal representation if they failed to collaborate! It also removes any possible incentive for an attorney to allow the collaboration to fail.

The team's goal is to help the parties to reach an agreed upon settlement that can work for the family. Although each attorney is representing one of the parties, and is charged with looking out for their interests and negotiating on their behalf, they are also working as part of the team. There is no room in collaborative process for the "barracuda" type of attorney who has a "winner take all" and "anything goes" mentality. The attorneys drawn to collaborative practice have often had extensive experience in the adversarial approach, and no longer want to be part of the destruction it causes. Although some will still take adversarial as well as collaborative clients, perhaps through financial necessity, many have given up their adversarial practices entirely.

The therapists who function as divorce coaches are both familiar with the family law system and experienced in dealing with the conflicts that occur within relationships. They will use their knowledge and experience to help their clients work through the intense emotions that often accompany divorce, deal with their hurt and anger, and face the reality that a negotiated settlement has to involve compromise and is not the place to "get even". Each party will have one attorney and one divorce coach who is working with them, but in frequent and regular contact with the attorney and divorce coach for the other party.

The child specialist and financial specialist are considered "neutrals", in that they represent neither party, but work independently: one to connect with and report on the needs and preferences of the children; and the other to provide an independent report on the estate and support issues, and assistance in finding ways to divide things fairly.

Meetings occur in different combinations. Each party might have some meetings with only their attorney or their divorce coach, but there are also 4-way meetings where the parties meet together with both attorneys (or sometimes both coaches), and sometimes six way meetings, where both parties, both attorneys, and both divorce coaches are in the room together. There may also be meetings with both attorneys and both divorce coaches, but without the parties present. The child specialist and financial specialist report and attend as needed. By working together, with a commitment to a negotiated solution, the team helps the parties to navigate both their differing needs, preferences and beliefs about what "should" be, and the hurt and angry feelings that so often accompany a divorce, in order to arrive at a workable solution that both can agree to.

Sometimes, when confronted with the number of experts involved and the expense of hiring these additional team members, there is a temptation to try to avoid that expense by just hiring attorneys to negotiate. Without the full team, however, the chances of successfully negotiating an agreement are significantly reduced, resulting in a much greater likelihood of ending up in the adversarial process, with all its added costs and long term negative implications. Experience has shown that working with the full collaborative team is likely to result in a better outcome and reduced costs, both financially and emotionally.

Collaborative Divorce is indeed more expensive than simple mediation, which, as stated previously, is the least expensive method of a professionally handled divorce. Not every couple, however, is able to mediate successfully. Sometimes one or both of the parties is just too stuck in their hurt and anger, or in their demands for what they believe they are entitled to, or finds it too difficult to trust their former partner even when he or she is making a sincere effort, to arrive at a workable solution with just a mediator. Collaborative practice, however, can enable all but the most dysfunctional couples to achieve a peaceful divorce. The power in this method is through the team approach, with each party feeling confident in the support of their own attorney, helped to work through their feelings by their divorce coach, and encouraged to look realistically at their situation by the entire team.

The net result financially, although costing more than mediation, is usually less than half that of adversarial litigation, and sometimes only a small fraction of litigation's long term costs. It is the outcome of the collaborative process, though, that is what's really important, far more so than the likely financial savings. While litigation often results in angry parties who feel victimized by the process, are waiting for the chance to get even or go back to Court for another try, and might be uncooperative and hostile, a divorce accomplished through the collaborative process is more likely to result in a relatively peaceful solution in which both parties have some investment, and are much more likely to follow through for effective and cooperative co-parenting. It is also far less likely to result in repeated complaints to the Court or the police, or additional legal procedures.

Some high conflict cases are eventually assigned to a "Special Master", an attorney or therapist who acts much like a judge, talking to the parties each time there is a conflict, reporting to the Court, and making recommendations that are most often implemented by the Court. This is likely to happen when, after an intense, painful and generally expensive divorce, often including a full custody evaluation, the couple is still unable to learn to co-parent together cooperatively. It becomes an ongoing expense, likely adding many thousands of dollars to the already considerable divorce costs. Even this may not keep the parties from returning to Court time and time again, fighting over every imaginable issue and possibly undergoing additional custody evaluations. The cost of this kind of divorce can go into six figures, and be a never ending source of conflict and stress for the parents. ***It is also a disaster for the children!*** The irony is that the kinds of solutions that are eventually imposed could easily have been arrived at collaboratively, if the parties had only been able to put aside their animosity and become willing to negotiate realistic compromises.

Adversarial

My views of the adversarial process should be pretty obvious by this point. It is the most expensive and stressful form of divorce, the one least likely to result in a solution that both parties can feel comfortable with, and the one likely to hurt the children most severely. Frequently, in fact, neither party feels good about the final decree, and each may feel victimized and resentful. The children also suffer the most in the adversarial divorce, having the trauma of their home being torn apart magnified many fold by the ongoing conflict between their parents. While each parent is likely to feel (possibly with some justification) that they are being victimized by the other parent, it is the children who are the actual victims of both. They will continue to suffer from the parents' animosity and lack of ability to co-parent cooperatively, and be continually traumatized, over and over again, by the conflict.

The adversarial process is the traditional way of divorce in our society, often with each party getting support for trying to "win", to get as much as they can, and give as little as possible to the other party, who they may see as having victimized them. It is my belief that no one wins through the adversarial procedure, except for the attorneys who profit from it, and perhaps the therapists who help the parents and their children recover from the effects of the conflict!

There are, however, a limited number of situations where an adversarial procedure might, in fact, be necessary. This tends to happen if there has been severe and one sided domestic violence, often in the classic "power and control" mode by one of the parties, or there are serious and *substantiated* allegations of molest or other child abuse or neglect. If one of the parties genuincly needs to get a restraining order against the other, to protect either themselves or their children, then a mediated or collaborative solution is unlikely. It is important, however, to distinguish between those situations where abuse has truly happened, and the all too frequent occasions where allegations may be either a projection or deliberate manipulation to maintain control by one of the parties, or the abuse has been mutual!

As a therapist, I know that the fact that a restraining order has been requested, and possibly granted, does not necessarily mean that domestic violence or child abuse has actually occurred! Likewise, allegations by one of the parties going through a painful divorce does not necessarily mean those allegations are true. Therapeutic help for the parties that can encourage more accurate reality testing, and support the choice of working together cooperatively, might well enable them to move from an adversarial procedure to a peacefully negotiated one. One of the dangers that well meaning therapists can fall into is to assume that an allegation of abuse or domestic violence made during a relationship breakup means that the abuse or violence has actually happened, and encourage and support actions that will lead to involvement of the legal system and a high conflict divorce, rather than helping their client with reality testing and looking at ways he or she can lessen the conflict by changing their part in it!

Another situation where there might be no way to avoid an adversarial divorce is where there is a large enough estate involved that greed takes over, and at least one party is dedicated to getting (or keeping) what most reasonable people might feel is more than their fair share. In this situation, the financial cost of the adversarial divorce might be far less than the estate at stake. Unless the parties can be motivated to let go of this and work out something reasonable, an adversarial divorce is likely. This will typically happen in celebrity divorces. Unfortunately, although the parties can afford the adversarial divorce financially, if there are children involved they will still suffer emotionally as the battle between their parents drags on, sometimes painfully in full view of the public.

In these situations, there is usually at least one party that is unwilling or unable to deal with the realities of their situation in a productive way. The other party, then, is forced to fight back to defend themselves, or flees (leaving the children to grow up without one of their parents). With two reasonably functional and mature adults, this should never happen, and *peaceful divorce should become the rule rather than the exception.*

Chapter Eight: Effective Co-Parenting

The Importance Of Cooperative Co-Parenting

It seems far too common for couples who are divorcing to believe they will never have to deal with their partner again after the divorce. This may be true when there are no children, since an estate can sometimes be divided in such a way that there is no need for the former partners to be in contact with each other after the divorce is final. Even alimony, if it is part of the divorce settlement, can often be handled in a lump sum arrangement that will eliminate the need for any further contact, or be set up to allow for automatic payments. When children are involved, however, this is not the case!

Children need and want both parents in their lives. For the children, two of the biggest impacts of the divorce are the loss of the stability that comes from the family being together as a unit, and the loss of time with each of their parents. Even when one of the parents works during the day, and the children only see him or her at night, there is still a certain security of knowing that mom or dad will be home at some point. When a divorce arrangement allows the children frequent and continuing contact with each parent, and to experience the parents as remaining a team to parent them, then much of the negative impact of the divorce can be mitigated.

If, however, one parent disappears from the children's lives entirely, becomes an occasional visitor who no longer seems part of the family, or just comes around every couple of weeks to take the children out for the day but is not a significant part of their daily lives (the stereotypical "Disneyland Dad"), then the long term outlook for their recovery from the divorce is far more problematic. This is also true if the children experience the parents as unable to work together in any way to care for them, perhaps unable to even be in the same room without fighting. Research has shown that the likelihood of significant ongoing negative effects of the divorce, including depression, anxiety, social and behavioral problems, and difficulty in relationships as an adult, increases dramatically with the loss of a parent or the inability of the parents to cooperate in a friendly manner.

It is therefore essential for the health and well being of the children that both parents remain fully involved in their children's lives, support the children having significant time with their other parent, and are able to handle exchanges in a peaceful and dignified manner. It is always best if the parents can deal with their differences and disagreements peacefully, but if they can't, it is essential that any conflict be kept away from the children. Parent's don't have to always agree with each other, and children can know that they have different values and outlooks. What is important, though, is that these differences be handled respectfully. Neither parent should ever involve the children in their disputes, never put the other parent down to the children, and never use them as a messenger to carry controversial, angry messages or demands to the other parent. Children used as pawns by their parents to express their conflict with each other are likely to suffer significantly from it!

This is sometimes the hardest part of the divorce. When one or both of the parents have the hurt and angry feelings so common during a relationship breakup, when they feel betrayed by their partner, abandoned, rejected, and treated unfairly, the last thing they may want to do is to have to get along peacefully with their former spouse. It is also easy, when caught up in wanting to get even, to want to keep "their" children away from that "terrible" ex-partner who treated them so horribly! It takes a measure of maturity and rationality, and the ability to put the children's needs first, not always easy things to come by during the stress of a divorce, to be able to put aside these angry feelings in order to co-parent successfully.

Of the many reasons for choosing a peaceful divorce over an adversarial one, the most important is to allow for successful co-parenting after the divorce. When agreements can be reached, and the ending of the marital relationship is handled peacefully, then co-parenting is far easier and less painful. After a high conflict adversarial divorce, it can be extremely difficult for the warring parties to switch back from the role of combatants to that of parents. The additional hurt and anger that the adversarial divorce process has added to the already considerable pain that was likely there before the divorce, may make it almost impossible to do so for quite some time. And yet, even after an adversarial divorce, the children's needs for each of their parents in their lives, and their need to experience their parents as a cooperative parenting team, is every bit as strong. In fact, if they have experienced the effects of the divorce conflict, unfortunately an all too common scenario, it is likely even more important!

Negotiating As Equals – Working As Partners

One of the key principals to successful co-parenting is to put aside the power struggles that may have gone on during the marriage or developed during the divorce. The parent who had primary responsibility for caring for the children during the marriage may feel that they are essentially "his" or "her" children, and that any time with the children or control over their upbringing given to the other parent is a loss to be fought against. Conversely, the parent who has been the primary provider, and may be paying child support, may well believe that his or her support payments give entitlement to be in control and make the decisions.

If, during the marriage, one of the parents tended to make final decisions in the family, they may well expect to continue that role after the divorce. Depending on the family structure and cultural heritage, this might have been either the parent who primarily cared for the children or the primary provider who brought in most of the income. In either case, any attempt to maintain that same level of control after the divorce will likely run into significant resistance. It is important for both parents to recognize that conditions have changed drastically, and new rules now apply. This can be especially difficult when it goes against cultural norms that the parent has learned and believes are "right".

Only by negotiating with each other as equals will the parents succeed in co-parenting successfully. Neither parent, after a divorce, is likely to tolerate behavior toward themselves that feels disrespectful or controlling. It may be hard for either of them to let go of control, but even when willing to do that, they will likely remain highly sensitive to any hint of the other parent taking over that control.

There are a few basic but essential keys to healthy co-parenting negotiations. One is to recognize that while each parent has control over what the children do when in their care, neither has solitary control over major decisions about the children, and therefore such decisions have to be arrived at through discussion and compromise. (This may not technically apply if one parent has full legal and physical custody, but that is typical only in fairly drastic situations, ones in which co-parenting might not be realistic anyway, and not the kind of divorce we are addressing here. Even in this instance, although the primary parent may have a Court ordered legal right to make these decisions themselves, it is still to everybody's advantage to make every effort to include the other parent as much as possible and learn to co-parent together).

Likewise, neither can dictate to the other how to raise the children when they are in their care, what rules to apply or how to apply them. The only influence they can have is through developing a spirit of working together as partners, where each one learns to hear the other, each learns to express their needs and beliefs in ways the other can hear, and differences are handled with mutual respect.

If your co-parent comes to trust that their requests to you will be treated with respect, and that they have some ability to influence (not control!) how you parent your shared children, it provides an incentive for them to reciprocate so that you will continue to behave that way and they will not lose what influence they have. On the other hand, if they experience you as turning a deaf ear to them and not caring at all about their concerns, they will also tend to reciprocate that attitude. Either approach is likely to create a positive feedback loop that helps to reinforce that behavior!

Respect is the key to successful negotiation! In the adversarial divorce, the parties generally experience the other parent (and possibly that parent's attorney) as treating them with little or no respect, not caring about their needs or beliefs, and trying to impose a solution that might seem totally unacceptable. When people feel disrespected by someone, and believe that that person has little concern for their needs or feelings, they get into a posture of defensiveness, and a readiness to do battle to protect their interests. The objective observer, talking to each of the parties in a high conflict adversarial divorce, would in all probability hear a passionate and convincing tale of victimization of that party by the other! The irony here is that, as the conflict escalates, there will likely be increasing truth in the complaints of victimization by both parties!

In order to co-parent successfully and negotiate productively, each parent must develop trust that their needs and desires will be taken seriously, that they will be treated with respect, and their positions will be considered respectfully even when disagreed with. This is typically a challenging place to get to after any divorce, but infinitely more so after a high conflict, adversarial, one. ***What is important here is to always remember that peace between the parents starts with treating each other with respect!***

Each parent may strongly believe they are "right" as to how to parent. While it is perfectly OK and even desirable to tell the other parent what you believe, it is important that they know you will also hear what they believe. When these beliefs are drastically different, and neither is likely to be influenced by the other's arguments for why their approach is right, then continuing to try to convince each other, or insisting on your "correct" way, will do nothing but increase hostility and make agreement more difficult. It is not necessary to agree with each other, or to pretend that you do, but it is necessary to let go of insistence and move into a posture of negotiation and compromise. Although it can be helpful to the children when there are similar rules and standards in their two homes, they are able to understand that those rules may differ, and can adapt to having different rules with each parent far more easily than to hostility and conflict between the parents.

Resolving Issues — Maintaining A Productive Co-Parenting Attitude

Having differences that need to be resolved in co-parenting is inevitable. What is important is how those differences are handled. Since by this time it is hopefully obvious that neither parent will be able to impose their preferred solutions on the other, it is only through a dialogue that each gets to feel truly part of that productive solutions can be arrived at.

The attitude with which the parents enter into this dialogue sets the basis for the ensuing negotiations. If either parent enters the discussion with the intention of demanding their way or insisting that their co-parenting partner agree with them, the process is almost certain to fail. If, however, both are able to put aside whatever tendencies they may have to do this, and enter into a discussion of equals with an initial expectation of compromise and mutual agreement, then success is likely. That doesn't mean that such discussions might not be challenging, but the right attitude by the parents from the very beginning will promote healthy rather than antagonistic debate, one which is likely to eventually produce an agreement acceptable to both. In the next chapter, Effective Communications, I will explore some of the techniques that can help smooth the way in negotiations.

Chapter 9: Effective Communications

Active Listening and "I-Messages"

In order to have a productive discussion, each parent must experience being heard by the other. This involves their being able to take turns during the discussion, giving each other a chance to speak, and making a reasonable attempt to consider and deal with each other's views. It is often productive for each to reflect back to the other what they think they have heard before answering, and only going on after the other parent agrees that they have been heard accurately. This process, known as active listening, can go a long way to helping defuse the feelings each may have of not being heard or understood, and facilitate improved communication. It is especially important to move into this technique any time the discussion is getting heated. It is also important to set aside adequate time to discuss difficult issues, when neither parent feels rushed and the children are not present.

It is essential for each to talk about their needs, desires, beliefs of what is right, etc. in ways that own that these ideas are theirs, and not put them out as a universal truth (even if they believe it is!). Statements such as "this is what I would like", "this is what seems best to me", "I believe this would be the best solution for…", etc. are much more effective than any statement that implies that your solution is the only way to do it, and any other ideas are nonsense to be dismissed. This is especially effective if you finish your statement by then asking your co-parenting partner what they think!

Statements to be avoided are those that can be seen as dismissive, demeaning, critical, or as any form of insult. A simple "How could you…" or "that's ridiculous", let alone an obvious putdown like "how can you be such a(n) _____", is likely to turn a discussion into a fight, and prevent any constructive solution from being arrived at. So can a sarcastic comment, or one said in a negative or sneering tone of voice, or while rolling your eyes. This is not to say that everything always has to be all smiles, and emotions have to be stifled. If you're feeling hurt or angry, that feeling can be stated gently, often with what are called "I-messages".

An I-message is a respectful way of communicating what you experience and how you feel about something. It has three basic parts, and an optional fourth part.

1. First is a statement of what the behavior is that you are having a reaction to. It might be stated as "When you..." followed by the event you are having feelings about. It could be put out as either an ongoing situation, i.e. "When you say to me...", or "When you don't...", or as a onetime incident, i.e. "When you said...", or "When you (whatever occurred...)". The important thing here is that you are talking about a specific behavior (doing or saying something or failing to do something) that bothers you.

2. The second part is a statement of feeling. This would normally be put out as "I feel...", or in the instance of a onetime happening, "I felt...". Keep in mind that any statement that begins "I feel that...", "I feel like...". "I feel as if...", or "it seems that" is NOT a statement of feelings, but rather a perception or belief. It still might be OK to use a statement like this, but it will need a genuine feeling statement to complete it. It is

also important to be sure that the perception or belief expressed is not put out in a way that can be taken as an insult. Saying something like "I feel that you were wrong to say that" or "I feel like what you did was harmful to..." might be OK, saying that "I feel that you're irresponsible" or "I feel that your doing that was stupid" would probably end any productive discussion!

To give you a better idea of how this might sound, let's put the first two statements together in some examples. "When you told... that..., I felt hurt and angry", or "When you forgot to..., I felt concerned about the consequences", or "Whenever you..., I feel dismissed and resentful", or "When you said..., I felt that you were not taking me seriously, and felt really angry at you". Note that the last statement includes a perception (I felt that), but also includes a genuine feeling statement (felt really angry). In addition, the perception is put out in a way that, although the other party might dispute the truth of it, is not likely to be seen as demeaning. These are all good feeling statements, that will make it easier for your co-parenting partner to hear your perspective and learn what you consider important.

One more point here is that it is essential to own your feelings rather than attribute them to the other person. Saying "when you..., I feel angry" is very different than saying "when you ..., you *make me* angry". The first is relatively easy to hear, the second is likely to result in defensive behavior and a probable argument. Someone's behavior may result in your feeling a particular way, it can "leave" you feeling that way, but it NEVER "makes" you feel that way. This is an important distinction for avoiding conflict. Since saying "makes me feel..." is a common expression in our culture, it becomes important to use conscious awareness to change our style to one less likely to exacerbate any conflict!

3. The third part of the I statement is the request. What is it that you would like to be different. This should be stated in a way that clearly comes across as a request, not as a demand or order. A request might be phrased "I would like it if, in

the future, you would …", or "I would prefer that you …", or possibly "I would appreciate it if …" or "it would feel better if…". There are many ways it could be phrased, but the important thing is that it is clearly a respectfully stated request.

4. The fourth, optional part, is a possible reciprocation. This is not always applicable, but in some situations can be helpful. For instance, someone who feels that they need some time to reflect before talking about a disagreement, talking to a partner who feels an urgency to deal with it immediately, might make an I statement that could go something like this: "When you want to discuss something and insist on my doing it immediately, I feel pushed and then feel defensive and angry. I need some time to cool off before we continue, and if you could give me that, then in return, I could agree to continue the discussion… (at a specific time, perhaps in an hour or two, or later that evening.)" This is an actual situation I have seen come up many times in couples counseling sessions, and the ability for each to state what they want, hear how the

other feels, and explore options together can be very productive in diffusing their conflicts.

Positions and Needs

When we are not getting what we need or are feeling threatened, it is typical to come up with some solution that we believe could change the situation to a more positive outcome. We may come to the conclusion that "if (the other parent) would agree to...", then everything would be OK. This, then, is likely to become our "position", in other words what we take into any discussion or negotiation. That position is not identical to our needs, but it is the way we have ***assumed*** our needs can be met. It is not unusual for two people who are struggling to resolve an issue between them to each get stuck in their positions, and to argue for those positions as if it is the only way their needs can get met. Sometimes, the positions might seem irresolvable because they may be diametrically opposed to each other.

If we can step back from our positions, and get in touch with the underlying needs and concerns, it is often far easier to find a negotiated solution than when each is coming from being locked into a position. An important part of this is to realize that there may be more than one way to meet our needs. By talking openly with our co-parenting partner about those needs and concerns, while giving them space to talk about *their* needs and concerns, it gives us a chance to explore creative ways that will allow each to address what they perceive their needs to be, and for each to be able to meet, if not all of what they need, at least most of it.

Unfortunately, by the time a couple has gotten to the point of divorce, it is often hard for each to trust the other enough to be vulnerable and back off their positions. When I am working as a mediator or doing co-parenting counseling, I try to help each parent learn to get in touch with and articulate their underlying needs so that they can step back from their positions, and also to learn to hear, and reflect back, the needs that the other expresses. Once they are both able to do that, then negotiating a solution, while not necessarily easy, at least becomes possible. It also helps to re-focus them on the needs of their children, which can easily be forgotten in the parental power struggle!

Stating Your Positions

Just as in successful couples work, the two most important aspects of healthy co-parenting counseling are learning to communicate with each other effectively, and learning to negotiate differences in a respectful way. The first step in communicating effectively is to be able to state what you want in a way that will not incite the other parent or feel like an attack on them. What many people often forget is that a prerequisite for doing this is to first be clear in your own mind what it is you want and what your reasons are for wanting it! Only then is it possible to give that information to the other parent. This is sometimes more difficult after an adversarial divorce, especially an extremely high conflict one, where real values around what a parent might believe best for their children, or want in order to make things easier in their own lives, can become confused with the feelings of defensiveness and hostility that may still linger.

Sometimes, if a parent is having difficulty getting clear on what it is they really need, then working on it with their individual therapist, or doing some individual sessions with the co-parenting counselor (with the agreement of the other parent) can help them to separate real needs from habitual reactions or unfinished issues coming up. Once clear about what they want, then using I messages and active listening to communicate with their co-parenting partner will allow each of them to feel heard and understood, and to develop a reasonably accurate idea of what is important to the other parent.

Learning To Mediate Differences

When a healthy and functional communication has been established, and each parent is able to state what it is they want and why they want it, understand what the other parent wants and why, and reflect back to the other parent what they have said in a way that allows the other parent to feel heard and understood, then the actual process of effective negotiation can begin.

Sometimes a parent may feel frustrated that they have clearly stated a position that seems obvious to them, have had it reflected back accurately, but the other parent "stubbornly" refuses to agree, and continues to maintain a conflicting strategy for the children. The danger here is in assuming that your position is so "obvious" that if the other parent does not agree they are being deliberately obstructionist, selfish or simply have no understanding of parenting. Although these **could** be possibilities, they are most often unlikely to be what is actually happening.

More likely, there is a genuine disagreement, and two people with the same facts are coming to different conclusions. To understand how common and normal this is, just look at the political partisanship happening at almost every level of government. The danger, whether in politics or in a family, is to assume something negative about those who disagree, such as ill intent, stupidity, greed, or selfishness. This is an all too common but counterproductive response on the political scene, and is even more destructive in a family, whether intact or dealing with co-parenting after divorce!

Mediating differences starts with each treating the other's positions with respect even when disagreeing with them, and then learning to differentiate their positions from their underlying needs and concerns and communicating those to each other. While not guaranteeing a solution will be found, this makes one much more feasible.

When needs and concerns are clearly stated by each, and each has understood the other's needs and concerns, very often a creative solution will emerge with relative ease.   If this doesn't happen, then the parents will need to engage in some degree of bargaining. This is a normal process, but is dependent on each letting go of any self-righteous "rightness" they may believe they have, as well as letting go of any sense of entitlement based on past history. These can both be difficult to do, but are essential for a constructive dialogue.

Compromise

When two people have differing needs as well as differing beliefs and values, and strongly disagree on an issue, a workable solution almost always involves some sort of compromise. The discussion often starts with each one trying hard to convince the other why their solution is the best and should be accepted by the other. Although there are times that one person may, after hearing what the other has to say, decide they can let go and agree with the other, much of the time that simply does not happen.   Often, the best that can be expected is that each will understand the other's position a little better, and may be able to move somewhat in the other's direction, but not enough to reach agreement. In these cases, it becomes essential to be able to negotiate a compromise.

This can be especially difficult when it comes to parenting, where it is natural to want to protect our children, and we are instinctively prepared to fight vigorously on their behalf. What couples in this situation need to realize is that, no matter how strongly they may believe they are right, the other parent probably feels just as strongly that **they** are right. In reality, it is not unusual for each to have some degree of reasonableness in what they are asking for. In addition, even if one party were more "right" than the other, and could somehow force the other parent to agree, whatever good for their child that might come out of this would likely be more than made up for by the harm to the children of their parents fighting!

The process of working out a compromise begins with each parent recognizing that a stalemate has been reached and that some form of negotiated compromise is necessary, and then clearly stating what they want, while also listening to (and actually hearing) what the other has to say. When this is difficult, active listening and "I statements" can be valuable tools to use, especially when combined with talking about needs rather than positions. Sometimes, it can be appropriate, and even helpful, to ask the other parent questions about what they want, as long as those questions are genuine requests for information, and not, as it is so easy to fall into, implied criticisms. "How could you..." is an obvious example of a question that is not a question at all, and is not likely to be received with an informative and respectful response!

A far better way might be to say, in your own words, something like "I'm finding it difficult to understand exactly why you want to..., and how you expect that to work out. Could you help me get a better sense of what you are thinking and what your expectations are?" Then **LISTEN** to the response with as open a mind as possible. You might well be surprised to find the other parent does have valid reasons, although it still might not be what you would choose. In addition, this kind of response makes it easier, if the other parent does see that their choices might have some problems, to own that rather than becoming defensive and argumentative.

There is a sign in a courtroom where I frequently attend meetings that points out that the words "listen" and "silent" are composed of the exact same letters. This is often a good thing to remember during this kind of discussion!

I don't mean to imply that this is an easy thing to do. It is, in fact, often one of the most challenging parts of co-parenting. However, it is important to recognize that as difficult as this may be, it is an essential part of learning to work together peacefully. You might not do it perfectly every time, but if you and your co-parenting partner both make a serious effort, and are honest about owning and trying to correct any lapses, then your communication will be off to a great start!

Once each parent has clearly stated how they see the situation, what they want, and *why* it is important to them (the underlying needs), then a discussion can begin on whether or not either can be comfortable agreeing to what the other is wanting. If not, as is often the case, then it becomes important here to begin to look for compromise solutions.

Middle Grounds, Creative Alternatives, Reciprocation

Negotiations most often involve finding some sort of middle ground. While they frequently begin with each party explaining their positions to the other, with all the justifications of why that should be the agreed on solution, when neither is able to fully convince the other, as is commonly the case, there has to come a point where each has to give up their chosen position and begin to explore how else things can be worked out. This, unfortunately, is where many couples get into trouble. It is essential to stay committed to the process, and not "pick up your marbles and go home" like an angry child might do, or to use the threat of doing that as a bargaining point!

As you might imagine, this brings us back to the issue I addressed somewhat earlier of **needs** versus **positions**. Even when our positions seem intractable and allowing no compromise, moving from demanding our positions to discussing our needs will open the door for the kind of creative thinking necessary to develop a workable solution.

If the parents have successfully been able to change the dialogue from rigid positions to a discussion of needs and concerns, very often even when they still disagree on an overall solution, at least some areas of agreement become apparent. Starting with these, a next step would be to explore possible middle grounds, areas where they can meet each other half way. Although this might not feel as satisfying to each as getting things done exactly the way they want, it is also a situation where no one loses, each has had input into the final result, and each gets some of what they want or believe to be right.

Many, if not most situations, can be resolved in this manner, but there are some that can't. Just as Solomon's suggestion to divide the baby in two would not have been a practical solution, there are some real life situations where a middle ground might seem to be doing just that; in other words, there does not appear to be any **workable** middle ground. In these situations, there are two other effective compromise techniques: exploring creative alternatives and asking for reciprocation.

Exploring creative alternatives involves looking at other ways to solve the problem that might have little or nothing to do with what either parent originally suggested. It is not a middle ground, somewhere between the parents' initial positions, but rather an exploration of ideas that might not have been initially obvious to either parent, but can come out of a cooperative mutual brainstorming session, or perhaps from input by a third party. The advantage of this is that an idea might arise that essentially meets each parent's needs, just from a different direction than either had anticipated.

The other option is a tradeoff, or asking for reciprocation. That means that one parent agrees to give in on one issue, in return for the other parent giving in on another, different issue. Although the negotiations on this can be longer and more complex than for the other methods, it is often the best way to turn a stuck place into a compromised agreement. It is important that the tradeoff is spelled out in advance, so it does not become a "blank check" that the parents are liable to end up arguing about later! Demanding one's way because "it's my turn", or "I gave in last time" is not likely to get the desired results if the other parent does not see it the same way. One advantage of this method of resolution is that not every issue has the same level of importance to each parent, and sometimes each can give in on the issue that is less important to them, resulting in what is effectively a win for both!

Whatever the method of negotiation, the discussion between the parents needs to go back and forth, with each taking the time to hear the other before replying, and each understanding that it will be necessary to accept less than what they might consider the ideal result. When an agreement is reached, it is important to spell it out in detail. It is only human nature, after spending time and energy struggling to come to a solution, to want to end the process as soon as possible and not have to put out any more energy or risk "rocking the boat". The difficulty with that, however, is that "the devil is in the details". If the compromise is left vague and not spelled out in detail, in makes it all too likely that at some future time each will interpret the agreement differently, will feel cheated by the other, and the conflict will begin anew. The way to avoid this is to be specific about the details of the agreement, even if it means extending a discussion that both wish could have been avoided!

It may sometimes be possible to work something out that is a hybrid combination of two or all three methods. This can be fine as long as both parents agree that the final resolution decided on is fair and equitable, and they are both willing to fully support the agreement.

Chapter 10: Developing Custody and Co-Parenting Plans

The Co-Parenting Attitude

Having a positive attitude toward negotiating, learning to listen to (and actually hear) each other, understanding the difference between our positions and our needs, and learning to work out compromises are all essential steps to developing a workable co-parenting plan. For many couples, this will be the most difficult issue they will ever have to negotiate. Each is likely to have different views of what is best for their children, and different priorities for them. In addition, any plan for shared parenting will of necessity involve less time for each parent than the experience of being a full time mom or dad before the divorce. This is true even for a parent who may not have been very involved in the children's lives before the divorce, but always knew that their children were there when they came home from work each evening. The awareness and acceptance of this reality is necessary, otherwise each parent will be feeling cheated by the other, with neither able to consider any reasonable compromise.

Parenting plans should start with an understanding that children need two loving parents in their lives. This is true no matter how hurt and angry one or both of the parents may feel. Each parent, in addition to having different beliefs as to what is good for their children, may also have different needs around scheduling. If the parents are working very different schedules, the most balanced parenting plan might look very skewed to the outside observer, but might be tailored to best meet the needs of each parent's schedule. One of the many advantages of working out your parenting plan rather than having the courts do it for you is the opportunity to be creative in developing something uniquely suited for your family's circumstances!

Some parents might want equally shared parenting, some might prefer having the children with them more than half of the time, and others might be content with a lesser amount of time that meets their needs for quality time with their children while respecting their particular work schedule. Obviously, when the needs or desires of the parents conflict around these issues, working out the details will be more challenging than when they complement each other. These are all things to be discussed and negotiated in developing the custody and co-parenting plan.

If the parents are working similar schedules, then there is likely to be a need for compromise around convenience. Additionally, it is important to remember that whatever periods of time a parent has the **right** to be with their children is also time that they are **obligated** to provide for their care. It is easy to forget that, although children may normally be in school for the day, in addition to having to deal with after school care there are also school holidays and days when a child is ill. The parent in charge during that time, although not necessarily having to be with their children personally during the entire time, must provide adequate supervision for them when they can't be. Knowing this in advance can help inject a dose of realism into the negotiations.

If there is a disagreement over the amount of time the children are to be in the care of each parent, this should be addressed first. If both parents want more than 50% of the children's time, (or if both would prefer less), or one wants more (or less) and the other wants an even sharing of time and responsibility, then it becomes important to engage in a productive dialogue as to their beliefs as to why the arrangement should be what they are requesting. It is essential here, since this can be an extremely delicate area, that the dialogue be constructive and respectful, with each parent truly listening to and hearing the other as well as presenting their own case in a clear and reasonable way. This is NOT a time to demand payback for previous "wrongs", or some form of imbalance to make up for a perceived imbalance of some sort during the marriage!

Although one or both parents may feel entitled to having more of a say, either because of having provided most of the actual care of the children during the marriage, or because of being the one providing most of the support or paying most of the bills, this is an attitude that will make productive negotiations difficult if not impossible, and will most likely result in a court battle instead of a negotiated agreement. Likewise a father who believes the "man of the family" should make the decisions, or a mother who believes it is "the mother's role" to decide about the children, has to readjust to the reality of shared parenting and negotiated agreements! This may be the most difficult adjustment of all, since these attitudes may well be supported by the parents' family, friends, and cultural background.

This is not to suggest that there might not be valid arguments for one parent or the other having more time with the children, especially at first. If the children are accustomed to spending most of their time with one parent, then a sudden transition to an equal share might not be the best thing for them. If one parent has a work schedule that lets them pick the children up from school at the end of the school day, but the other would have to leave the children in childcare several hours each day after school, this should also be taken into consideration. The important thing here is that both parents must understand that neither one, no matter how justified they think they are in what they are asking for, can dictate to the other or demand compliance. A negotiated agreement must be just that, **negotiated**! And that means between two parents meeting as equals, with neither one trying to overpower the other, something that can't be emphasized enough!

Shared parenting is far easier when the parents live near each other, preferably close enough so that the children can comfortably go to the same school from each house. Since the children will be attending one school during the school year, if the parents live too far away for the children to go to the same school from both homes, then a decision has to be made as to which parent the children will live with during the school week. Although for younger children in day care or preschool there can theoretically be two separate locations for child care, this is not likely to be a good idea, since the children will benefit from the consistency of having the same day care provider and companions for the entire week, rather than having to adjust to two different situations. Since this can seriously up the ante on any decision around shared parenting, I believe it is important that, if at all possible, neither parent move too far from the other for this to occur, and moves of any distance be negotiated between the parents. Although this does give each parent veto power over the other's right to move, at least when more than minimal distance is involved, and that is something that both parents may find hard to swallow, remember that, in addition to being mutual, it is **substantially** in the children's interest to have this arrangement.

In a separate publication on Mediation Agreements, which will be available on the website, "www. divorcingpeacefully.com", I will include sample custody and parenting plans with specific details as to possible arrangements. Those plans will be usable either as an actual template with only the specifics for the family needing to be filled in, or as a general guide for developing a unique parenting plan that best suits the family's circumstances. In this chapter, however, I will discuss these plans more in terms of general ideas. I will start with plans for equally shared parenting, then plans for parenting when the children will be spending more time with one parent, and then plans for situations where the parents live too far apart for the children to be able to commute to the same school from both homes. Lastly, I will address the most difficult and unadvisable situation, that in which one parent moves out of state, or even out of the country. Under these circumstances, a plan that provides adequate time for the children to be with each parent is normally impossible, and because of that, it is the situation most likely to result in prolonged court battles and custody evaluations, as well as being invariably detrimental to the children.

Issues In Co-Parenting

1. The first issue that needs to be decided between the parents is what the time share will be. If they agree on an equal sharing of time and responsibility, there are a number of different ways of working that out. If they decide, for whatever reason, that the children will spend more time with one of the parents, then it is important to have some idea of just what that means. Two parents might agree that one of them would be the primary parent, but one of the parents might see that as a 60-40 split of time, and the other might see it as 80-20! Before starting to work out the specific details, it is essential to have at least some agreement in principle on how the shared time will be divided. Although the court system shuns parenting arrangements based on percentages, and the final agreement has to spell out specific times rather than proportions or percents, in

my experience most parents initially think more in percents, often with no clear idea of what that might mean in terms of specifics.

2. A second issue is how transitions will occur. One of the easiest ways, for both the parents and the children, is to transition through school or day care; i.e. the parent the children are leaving drops them off at school, and the other parent then picks them up at the end of the day. It can often be worked out that most of the transitions will occur this way, but there will always be the need for some that involve direct transfer between the parents. This will most often occur on holidays or school vacations, or if a child is ill. For those cases, the time of transition should be an integral part of the agreement.

3. For instance, on a day where one parent normally drops a child off at school, possibly on the way to work, and the other picks them up at the end of the day, what happens on a school holiday, or if the child is ill? The parents could agree that transitions will take place in the morning as

if the child were being brought to school, that they could take place at the end of the day as if the child were being picked up from school, or, they could take place at a mutually agreed time in the middle of the day, perhaps around the half way mark. Any of these solutions would be equally valid, but they should be worked out at the time of the agreement, not negotiated on an ad hoc basis when the situation is occurring!

4. Another issue here is transportation. Most often, unless there is a reason to vary this, transportation is shared equally between the parents. Even here, though, there is still a question of how that is managed. The receiving parent could provide the transportation, the transferring parent might provide it, or some other way might be worked out that the parents specifically feel works best for them, such as meeting in the middle, somewhere between their two homes.

5. Holidays represent a variation from the normal schedule. The first thing to decide is what holidays are important to each parent. If

they each want the children with them on the same holidays, then the two common ways of sharing are either alternating years between them or finding a way to split the time on each holiday. For instance, in one family I worked with, Christmas eve was an important time to have the children but Christmas day less so for one parent, and the reverse was true for the other, mostly based on the extended family they traditionally spent each of those two times with. They were able to agree that one parent would always have the children on Christmas eve, and the other on Christmas day, and the only thing left then to negotiate around this was the actual time of transition. In this case, what was settled on was the night itself alternating between the homes, with half the time the transition being late evening Christmas eve, the other half it being early Christmas morning. This also allowed the children to continue to spend their holiday with the same extended family members they were used to in each case, clearly a plus for them, and an excellent example of a good compromise.

6. If the parents have different priorities, which might be especially true if they come from different religious traditions, the task is often easier, with each parent getting the children on the holidays that are most important to them. Even with parents of the same religion, one might prefer to have the children on religious holidays, and the other might prefer having them on, say, the Fourth of July and Memorial Day weekends. Any such arrangement that both parents can agree on and the children feel OK with is valid!

7. The various legal holidays and three day weekends, such as Labor Day and Memorial Day weekends, July 4th, Thanksgiving Day, etc. must also be accounted for in the sharing plan. To some families, who the children spend Halloween with is important, to others it may not be at all. The parenting plan should address each of the holidays that are significant to one or both parents. Other holidays that the parents don't particularly care about can be left on the normal schedule. In addition, the time

of transition for each holiday should be set in the initial agreement.

8. When co-parents are getting along fairly well, there may be a tendency to not want to be so specific, with both making the assumption that they will work out the transition time as it comes up. This may work out well **most of the time**, but it leaves the door open to escalated conflict on those occasions where each parent has a different priority, or makes different assumptions about what the agreement means. It is far better to set specific details in place, then agree to be as cooperative and flexible as possible as to its implementation. No one is going to insist on the parents following the letter of their agreement if they are both in accord on the actual arrangements. Remember, the agreement itself is really a "fallback plan" when the parents can work together comfortably with cooperation and flexibility.

9. A good custody/co-parenting plan should anticipate any possible future areas of conflict, and provide a solution. This will avoid

misunderstandings that might later come up, or situations where one parent's needs change and the original plan is now less comfortable for them.   It's great when parents can be flexible with each other and work cooperatively on an ongoing basis, but even here, the written agreement's fallback position will generally help to keep the situation cooperative, and prevent conflict from developing. I would suggest that even when being highly specific may seem unnecessary due to the degree of cooperation, it is still wisest to be specific in the written agreement, then choose to ignore it as long as both parents are able to agree. Something as simple as having different assumptions about the time of transition when a child is ill, or sharing transportation on the holidays, can throw the proverbial monkey wrench in the entire agreement, maybe even after years of working well.

10. What a fallback plan means is that, if there is a disagreement, either parent has the right to stick to the original written plan. Each can request

changes, and those changes can be negotiated, but **neither has the right to make changes unilaterally,** and if changes can't be agreed on, then the written plan takes precedence. This is true even if circumstances have changed. The rare occasions where the parents might disagree will prove the worth of having worked out the specific details in advance, since with either parent having the right to insist on the agreement, it will eliminate the likelihood of disagreements escalating into arguments. It also provides an incentive to be as flexible as possible so that the other parent will also be flexible, but with a safety valve for when that doesn't work. It is important, therefore, to create a strict agreement that covers all eventualities, even when the parents are normally able to work well together. Of course, when the parents are having difficulty working well together, it becomes crucial.

11. The summer schedule will normally be considerably different than that during the school year. Since the children are not likely to be

in school, there is the option to be more flexible about how the schedule is developed. Both parents are likely to want some time in which they can take their children on an extended vacation, and it is therefore necessary to decide for how long each parent can take the children, how many times during the summer this can be done, and how decisions will be made as to when each parent will have that option. When each parent needs to notify the other before a proposed vacation time, and what rights the other parent may have to object to the schedule (perhaps they were planning to vacation the same week, but hadn't yet provided notification to the other parent), should be spelled out. The transition times and transportation may be different over the summer, and this also needs to be addressed in the agreement.

12. In addition to working out the details of custody and time sharing, a parenting plan should also address how things are to be handled when there is disagreement. Sometimes that disagreement will come up over things that, for

whatever reason, have not been anticipated. One possibility is to give either parent the right to request co-parenting counseling or mediation, with the other parent being obligated to join them until either the problem is resolved or both parents agree to take a break from the counseling. Parents should also agree to be open and honest with each other. The terms of choosing to bring in outside help, and the way the specific professional will be chosen, should also be included in the agreement.

Plan Development

The first thing to be decided is how much time the children will be with each parent, as we covered above. Once that is established, then the specific days would be looked at next. Some typical arrangements for even sharing might be one week with each parent then switching, the first half of the week with one parent and then the second half with the other with alternating weekends, or, especially for younger children, a day or two with each parent and several transitions. There is value in not having the children away from either parent for too long a time, especially for younger children, but there is also something to be said for minimizing the number of transitions, which would mean longer times with each parent. Each family should carefully weigh the pros and cons of these conflicting options in light of their children's specific needs, personalities and developmental stages.

There is an often agreed on rule of thumb that suggests a child should not be away from either parent for more than one day per year of age. That would suggest a transition at least every two days for a two year old child, but that a four year old could handle half a week with each parent, and a child of seven or older could handle a week with each. This does not mean that these specific times of separation are essential, or even advisable, but that the child will likely be able to handle them without serious detriment to their attachment to the absent parent.

When parents are agreeing that the child will spend more time with one parent than with the other, there are several options for implementing this. One might be alternating weekends, but with the children being returned to the primary parent early Sunday evening on their weekend with the non-primary parent. Midweek days may be split so that one night of each week is spent with the non-primary parent, and the other nights with the primary parent. Another option, which might be especially relevant for younger children, or when the non-primary parent has not previously been very involved in the children's lives, would be one or two afternoons per week picking the children up from school and returning them to the primary parent sometime before bedtime. In such an arrangement, the parent spending the afternoon and early evening with the children would generally be responsible for providing dinner for them, and, in the case of older children who are likely to have homework after school, providing a place for them to do their homework and whatever assistance is appropriate.

In situations where the parents have drastically different schedules, sharing of custody can be implemented in any number of creative ways. If one parent works a night job while the other works days, the children might spend every afternoon and school holiday with the night working parent, but every night with the day working one. If one parent works weekends but is off some weekdays, then they might have the children with them on those weekdays, plus some evenings during the rest of the week, but leave them on weekends with the parent who doesn't work then. Although unusual situations of availability of one or both parents can be challenging to work out, the end result can be the children spending more actual time with each of their parents! Parents might also agree that if for any reason the parent whose custodial time it is isn't able to care for them personally at any time, the other parent would have first right of refusal to have the children with them, rather than their being left with a friend or partner, or put in day care. The important thing here is that all the implications and ramifications of the arrangement be discussed in full, and the final agreement be one that both parents feel comfortable with!

When the basic arrangement has been agreed on, the next step is to look at times the children are not in school. This would include summer vacations and regular school holidays. It would also include any special occasions, such as religious holidays, that are important to one or both parents. The most common way to share holidays is to alternate them, but sometimes splitting the time is preferred by the family. This is especially applicable for extensive holiday times, such as Winter or Spring vacations from school which may last a week or more. In general, the children are with their mother on Mother's Day and their father on Father's day, with the specific times worked out based on the family's preferences. Some families will also split time on the children's birthday, but this can make it hard for the child to celebrate and have a party, so often the parent who does not have the child with them on their actual birthday will celebrate with them the weekend before or after. Again, there is no simple rule on this, and any arrangement that is comfortable for both parents and also works for the children would be acceptable.

After agreeing to the days the children will be with each parent, the next thing to consider is the times of transfer and transportation. Most often, unless there is a specific reason otherwise, the parents share transportation. The parent receiving the children might pick them up, the parent delivering them might bring them, or each might take responsibility for specific times. Sometimes, if one parent finds the travel more difficult, there might be a negotiation where one parent provides most, or even all, of the transportation in return for some other tradeoff that can be an acceptable compensation.

Any of these arrangements can be workable, and they have different advantages and disadvantages. If children are having a hard time with transitions, I believe it can be better for the receiving parent to pick them up, since that way the transition happens at the home they are leaving, and they don't have to deal with a period of time during which they have effectively left one home, although still with that parent, and have not yet arrived at the home they are transitioning to. This arrangement will also minimize times where a parent who might have some difficulty keeping to a precise schedule will tend to be late, sometimes leaving the other parent steaming at their home waiting for their child to be dropped off, or, even worse, at a neutral pickup point. If the parent knows the other parent will be at their home at a certain time, they are more likely to have the child ready than they might be to arrive at the receiving parent's home in a timely manner.

At this point it would be appropriate to bring up the issue of promptness. No one likes being kept waiting, and this can be especially galling when it is a co-parent who does it, especially in the sensitive first years after the divorce when there may be many unfinished issues and any degree of cooperation is difficult. Whether bringing the children for drop-off or picking them up, it is important to make every effort to be on time, and if, on rare occasion, one is running a bit late, to promptly call your co-parent and let them know when to expect you. An occasional lapse, especially if it does not occur too often or for too long a time and is appropriately acknowledged and apologized for, can be forgiven; complete disregard of time commitments can put the entire custody and co-parenting agreement in jeopardy. When agreements break down and do eventually end up in court, consistent failure to arrive on time or have the children ready for pickup on time is often one of the first complaints made to the judge or custody evaluator!

Some families will prefer for the parent who is dropping the children off to provide the transportation. The advantage of this option is that parents do not always stay home with their children, but often take them places. When the receiving parent does the pickup, this means the parent the children will be leaving has to either return home, or call the receiving parent to arrange a new pickup point for that time. This can also be a source of conflict between two co-parents who have not yet fully made peace with each other, since the receiving parent may resent having to change, especially if it seems to be further, or in some way a more difficult drive, than to the other parent's home. For children who do not have a difficult time with the transitions, this can be a very workable alternative.

Sometimes, pickups are arranged at a neutral point. This is mostly appropriate when the parents find it difficult to be in each other's presence without fighting, and one or both parents does not want the other parent in their home. This arrangement is more common in a high conflict divorce when ordered by the court, but in some instances it may also be appropriate for a negotiated co-parenting situation that still has some unresolved antagonism between the parents. It is important to keep in mind, though, that this is far from an ideal solution, and can be uncomfortable for everyone, especially the children. The worst case scenario is when the "neutral" place is at a police station. Think about what this tells the children!

Ideally this would only be a temporary situation, and can evolve to one in which the exchanges normally occur at one of the homes the children live in, which is generally best for the children. It may also be appropriate, however, in situations where the parents live a considerable distance from each other, and instead of taking turns driving arrange a transition point between their homes, with each parent sharing half the driving for each trip.

One exception to shared transport is when one parent only visits the children, and they do not stay with that parent overnight. In that case, the visiting parent might both pick up and drop off the children. If the children stay with that parent on the weekends, but he or she just visits with them during the week, then the parent with primary custody may do more than 50% of the transport on those weekends to balance out not providing any transport during the weekdays. This is a situation that may be especially likely when the parents live too far from each other for the children to attend the same school from both homes, but not so far that a commute is impossible.

Frequently, when children attend school or daycare, it is possible to arrange most pickups and drop-offs to occur at that location. This is always preferable to a direct pickup or drop-off, since it provides a natural transition for the children and also lessens situations where conflict between the parents may come up. What is important is that the parents explore different options together, talk openly about what their preferences might be and why, and work out reasonable compromises about differences in what they each might prefer.

The situations where one parent has moved out of the area are the most difficult to work out peaceably, and represent a disproportionate number of high conflict cases and custody evaluations. No parent wants to be separated from their children for an extended period of time, even one who may not have previously been very active in their lives. To move far enough that the children cannot see both parents with some reasonable frequency is *never* in the children's best interest, even if there are other factors that might make the move a beneficial one for the parent. It is my belief, and to the best of my knowledge that of most therapists, custody evaluators, and judges, that except in the most extreme cases of severe domestic violence or child abuse, children need both parents and neither parent should be excluded from their children's lives.

It is important to understand that a parent who might well be willing to compromise and cooperate in deciding a parenting schedule is considerably less likely to do so when a move-away is involved. Choosing to relocate is almost a guarantee of a lengthy, expensive and emotionally draining court battle. Even a parent who might well be willing to settle for less than fully shared custodial time, and prepared to work together to co-parent cooperatively, is likely to fight vigorously against a relocation of their children. It is important that any parent considering a relocation after a divorce understand the ramifications of their actions, both as far as almost ensuring ongoing conflict, and being hurtful to the children no matter who they end up living with.

When one parent moves out of the area, especially when it is a distance of hundreds or even thousands of miles, no matter who has primary custody, the children lose.

Sometimes a parent is so angry at the other parent that they want to hurt them, want to punish them by taking "their" children, but the reality is that it is the children who are hurt most. In years past, the custodial parent, most often the mother, was given the right under the law to move anywhere and take the children with them. That has changed in the last decade or so, with legal precedent in California, for instance, that now considers the best interest of the children. Although the courts cannot order a parent not to move, it can, and sometimes does, order a change of custody based on the parent moving, and remove the children from the parent who chooses to leave.

There are several factors that can lead to this. One is that, assuming the children have a reasonably good relationship with each parent, they are likely to also have multiple connections in the area they have been living. There is likely to be a school they are familiar with, friends they spend time with, and possibly other relatives or friends of the parents who are active in their lives. They may also attend religious services and/or religious school locally, and perhaps have been members of a congregation one or both parents have belonged to. Since the court is likely to see it in the children's interest to maintain as much stability as possible during a time of difficult transition, this is likely to influence the court towards the parent remaining in their jurisdiction. The court and/or evaluator may also see the willingness of one parent to move to a location that inevitably will seriously disrupt the children's relationship with one parent or the other as an indication of not putting the children's needs first, again influencing them further in the direction of the parent who is not moving.

Even in instances where one parent has limited custody due to substance abuse problems, the courts will generally look to help that parent, if they go through rehabilitation, have therapy, and become clean and sober, to gradually move toward more custodial time with their children. The same is true of a parent that has had their time with the children limited due to child neglect or a moderate degree of domestic violence or child abuse: therapy and parenting classes, and a good track record during the limited (and possibly supervised) visitation time, will result in gradually increasing time for the improving parent. (Severe child abuse or domestic violence is another matter entirely, and could result in more drastic consequences for the offender, including, in the most extreme cases, even going as far as loss of parental rights!

This is not to say that custody will automatically be awarded to the parent who is not relocating. There are many circumstances that need to be taken into account, including the kind of relationship each parent has with their children, how responsible and stable each is seen to be, if either has had any verified problems with substance abuse, domestic violence, or child abuse or neglect, if either has any kind of arrest record, etc. What is important to know, however, is that the moving parent is likely to have to demonstrate a considerable benefit to the children from being with them to overcome the detriment of the move. Even then, they should realize that it is primarily the children who will be paying the price for their decision to relocate!

It is not uncommon for a custody evaluator, in the case of a prospective move-away, to offer two alternate recommendations, one to occur if the moving parent actually does move and an alternate one if they decide to stay within local commuting distance of the other parent. The first recommendation might give custody to the parent not moving, with visitation to the relocating parent appropriate for the distance to be traveled and ages of the children, and the alternate recommendation may be a much larger share of custody, possibly fully shared or even primary custody, if the parent does not relocate.

If parents do try to negotiate around a move-away, it might involve alternating years with each parent, or letting the children choose each year who they want to live with for that school year. Most often, in a case like this, the parent with whom the children don't live during the school year will have them most of the summer, and possibly most holiday time during the school year. They are also likely to have the right to visit with the children any time they choose to travel to where the other parent lives, including spending long weekends with them, and possibly having the children with them for a week or two if they are able to provide a suitable location for them to live during that time.

This is not a good solution for the children, but once a move-away takes place, it is probably the best that can be hoped for. Before considering the move, it would be a good idea to seriously explore other possible options which may have less negative impact on the children, and be less likely to generate conflict.

Chapter 11: Recovering From Adversarial Divorce

Difficulties In Getting Back On Track

It is important to know that it is never too late for parents to begin to learn to work cooperatively for the benefit of their children. Even when the family has suffered through the pain and expense of an adversarial divorce, transitioning from a position of mutual hostility to one of cooperative co-parenting will always be of significant benefit to the family, especially to the children. When divorced families maintain an ongoing position of hostility between the parents, the actions of each parent tend to hurt and anger the other parent, creating the constant potential for escalation. This creates a crazy situation for both of the parents, but as always is most devastating to the children. The sooner the parents can learn to put aside their anger at each other and become effective co-parents together, the better it will be for the children, as well as easier for the parents themselves.

This is not to suggest that this is an easy thing to do after a high conflict adversarial divorce, especially one that had a custody evaluation and possibly antagonistic allegations by each parent about the other. There will inevitably be some emotional scarring from the battles, and often a desire to "get even", or at least to protect oneself against the other parent. Frequently, the most difficult time for the divorcing family in an adversarial divorce is **after** the final decree is issued, when the level of hostility between them may be at a maximum, and passive aggressive resistance to following the order, or even outright disobedience of it, may occur.

Taking The First Steps

If, however, the two parents are truly concerned about the best interest of their children, then this is a time to begin the process of reconciliation as parents, and learning to work together to co-parent. In many cases, the Court will order co-parenting counseling for the parents to try to facilitate this process. Even if this is not the case, it is advisable that the parents agree to work together with a co-parenting counselor to assist them in learning to cooperate in parenting their children.

A good co-parenting counselor will understand that this is a difficult process for the parents, who may be filled with hostility toward each other and have difficulty being in the same room without descending into conflict. It may sometimes be necessary to meet individually a few times with one or both of the parents during this process in order to help them deal with their feelings about the other parent and give them some reality testing about the effects of their actions. If the parents are in personal therapy, generally a good idea when dealing with the stress of a divorce, especially a high conflict one, then coordination between the co-parenting counselor and any individual therapist(s) can be extremely helpful.

In order for this process to be effective, both parents must accept the reality that cooperative co-parenting is important for their children, and become willing to put aside their own hurt and anger to make it work. Until this happens progress is impossible, and either parent can sabotage the process. Once the parents both realize that learning to co-parent together is essential, and honestly commit themselves to it, then the actual work can begin. Each parent must learn how to state how they feel about a situation, how it affects them, what they believe is in the best interests of their children, and what they would like from the other parent, and to do so without attack or disparagement of the other parent. A parent may not like what the other parent is doing, may in fact feel appalled by it, but has to learn that it just doesn't work to talk about it in a way that will leave the other parent feeling attacked and delegitimized. Provoking a defensive reaction, the almost inevitable response to feeling attacked, will only get in the way of productive communication.

Likewise, it is important for each parent to learn to listen to the other, and to genuinely hear what their co-parent has to say. First of all, when we begin to understand where another person is coming from, it makes it easier to develop a sense of context for their actions and have a more realistic perspective on them. Secondly, when someone experiences being heard and understood, even when disagreed with, they become more able to engage in productive dialogue. If they do not experience that, they are more likely to intensely defend their positions. I address communications between the parents in detail in Chapter IX, Effective

Communications, which might be worth reviewing at this time.

The process of learning to co-parent together is very similar to the process of negotiating a custody and co-parenting agreement in the first place, but likely made much more difficult due to the hostility left over from the adversarial divorce. It is, however, no less important! Although starting out with a negotiated agreement and avoiding the adversarial process is always the better alternative, the saying "better late than never" certainly applies here. It will take time to undo the hurt to the family the high-conflict divorce has likely caused, but the sooner the process begins, the better off everyone will be.

The process can be complicated when the Court awards full legal custody to one parent. Although that parent then has the right to make decisions regarding the children on their own, doing so is likely to be continually seen by the other parent as discounting their role as parent, and will generally keep the parenting relationship in a state of ongoing conflict and hostility. To the extent that the custodial parent can let go of the power the Court has awarded them, and make reasonable attempts to include the other parent in their decisions, the process of working together will be facilitated. Since no matter who makes the decisions, both parents are likely to be involved in implementing them, and since the parents will still have to communicate regarding scheduling, school and homework issues, health issues, etc., sharing power in making decisions for the children can be a small price to pay for lowering the conflict. The part the non-custodial parent can play in this is to put out what they would like as a request, rather than as a demand, requesting it in a respectful way, and trying to avoid getting into an argument when they don't get their way no matter how justified they may feel!

The above clearly would not apply equally when the reason one parent was excluded from legal custody was due to severe child abuse, domestic violence, or substance abuse issues. In those cases, the custodial parent must first and foremost protect their children and themselves. Those are not, however, the only times a court may choose not to order joint custody, and it is the other situations I am talking about, the ones without a criminal level of abuse or violence or a danger to the children or custodial parent. Even in those extreme situations, there may well be some ways that the non-custodial parent can be included in parenting decisions, and in any event the need to communicate about the children makes co-parenting counseling even more essential.

Personal Counseling

A divorce, even a peaceful one, is one of the most difficult times in most people's lives. The grief over the loss of the relationship and the ending of the many hopes and dreams often attached to it, the loss of each partner's primary companion and main source of intimacy (this is often true even in relationships that have been difficult for a long time, including some that have edged on mutual violence), the inevitable loss of time with one's children and loss of one's role in the children's lives, the struggles over how to divide up the parenting "pie", and the need to deal with dividing property, all contribute to an often overwhelming amount of stress. Severe anxiety and depression are not uncommon in these situations.

As a psychotherapist dealing with a wide variety of clients, I have found that the majority of people who enter therapy for the first time do it in response to either severe stress in a relationship or the ending of one. They may initially come in for couples counseling to try to save the relationship, or after the relationship has ended to deal with depression, anxiety, loneliness, and a general feeling of being lost, but sometimes continue with significant, and frequently life changing, personal work.

Personal psychotherapy can make a significant difference in an individual's ability to handle these stresses. In some instances it can help to save a relationship, or let the couple renew it on new, and possibly more mature, terms. It is not uncommon that a couple will come into counseling being highly reactive to each other. Often, they will benefit mostly from individual therapy, where they can explore the dynamics of their reactivity, work through unfinished issues that are triggered by their partner, and then become open to exploring new ways of responding to each other. In these situations, it is usually best if both partners are doing individual work, but even if only one is participating, by learning to become aware of and contain their own reactivity, to communicate with their partner in a mature and healthy way, and to set boundaries appropriately and gently, they will often become able to influence how their partner responds to them, and make a significant difference in the relationship.

When a relationship has dissolved, the client often has to first deal with severe pain and grief before moving on to exploring other issues. These can include the kind of relationships they get into, what they may contribute to the problems, and how to both create healthier relationships for themselves and respond to their future partners in ways that will promote solutions rather than arguments. This is especially true in a divorce where there are children. As I stated previously, each parent loses some of the time they had experienced as being a parent, and the loss often feels devastating, maybe far worse than the loss of the partner they may have been fighting with for some time. Until their grief is resolved and worked through, any real progress, whether in therapy to deal with relationship issues or in their lives as a whole, is unlikely.

Considering this, I can't stress how important it is that anyone going through a divorce, especially with children involved, make the commitment to obtain some serious psychotherapy for themselves. This becomes even more true for adversarial divorces, especially high conflict ones. Similarly, children whose parents are going through a divorce should ALWAYS be taken to a therapist, even if they are not manifesting any visible symptoms. It is almost impossible for a child to not be seriously affected by their parents' separation, but some children can be very skilled at hiding their feelings, and this can cause them serious problems throughout their lives.

Considering the amount of money often invested in a divorce, especially the high conflict variety, the cost of therapy is relatively small, and the benefits are significant. It may also be possible to cover at least some of the cost of therapy through a parent's health insurance or Employee Assistance Program, and schools will also often provide counseling services for the children. However it is done, therapy will make a considerable contribution to helping the family move beyond the stress and pain of the divorce.

2868689

Made in the USA